WAIT

WAIT

Waiting on God in a World that Won't Wait

SMEDLY YATES

Kress Biblical Resources
www.kressbiblical.com

Wait: Waiting on God in a World that Won't Wait

ISBN 978-1-934952-21-4

Unless otherwise indicated, all Scripture is taken from the NEW AMERICAN STANDARD BIBLE®, Copyright © 1960, 1962, 1963, 1968, 1971, 1972, 1975, 1977, 1995 by the Lockman Foundation. Used by permission.

Throughout this work God's personal name, *Yahweh*, is used to reflect the Hebrew text. Many English versions of the Bible, including the New American Standard Bible, render the name Yahweh as "LORD." The significance of God's name will be explained further in Chapter 3.

Cover image by Sam Pagel, eightyeightproductions.com
Cover design, interior design, and typeset by Katherine Lloyd, theDESKonline.com

The Biblical Greek and Hebrew fonts are used with permission and are from BibleWorks (www.bibleworks.com). Copyright ©1994-2013 BibleWorks, LLC. All rights reserved.

For my Pop,
who waits for the resurrection in the presence of Jesus,
with all the saints who
"have slipped the surly bonds of earth"[1].

1949-2012

1   These words are borrowed from John Gillespie Magee, Jr., an American fighter pilot killed during World War II.

Many thanks to

My under-the-sun treasure, my wife and best friend, Janet; my mom, for encouraging me to write and offering many helpful corrections; the elders of Grace Bible Church, my pastors who serve God's people humbly and effectively; Becky Sitton, who tediously transcribed sermons for much of the content of this book; George and Jamie Siegele, who graciously lent their mountain retreat (and the glorious thunderstorms!) for writing; Cameron Dodd, without whose literary labors this book would have remained a clumsy jumble of words; friends who nudged me to write, and friends who took the time to read and correct cumbersome manuscripts—Brian, Pete, Jason, Jonathan; for David, Jr., who has taught me what it looks like to wait on God; and Rick Kress, who has kindly endured my attempt to put thought to print.

Contents

Introduction

Several years ago I read these words in my Bible: "Rest in the LORD and wait patiently for Him" (Psalm 37:7). Though I had read the words before, they seemed new to me. Here was a command from God to wait. I hated waiting. Waiting had always seemed like wasted time. Yet here was a command to do what was loathsome. I set out over the next year to explore everything God had to say about waiting on Him, for I clearly was missing something that was important to Him.

Discoveries far outpaced my expectations. I learned that waiting on God is not just doing nothing. Waiting on God is faith expressed in persevering obedience while trusting God to work all things according to His perfect plan in His perfect time; or put mathematically, waiting on God is trust multiplied by time. I discovered that waiting on God is a powerful weapon for the fight with sin in my own heart. Being forced to wait also reveals my heart's idols. Whenever I find that my circumstances won't change according to my desires, my impatience, worrying, or complaining demonstrate that my affections are misplaced, that I love some thing more than I love God. When I get so much as a cold, I grow impatient, longing to feel "normal" again. I put my hopes in feeling well, in an energetic return to my usual activities. My infrequent discomforts reveal my idolatry: I worship at the altar of a pain-free, comfortable existence.

I have friends with degenerative ailments who will not get better before they leave this life. They teach me every day what it means

my idolatry is that I want things my way now.

to wait on God. Rheumatoid arthritis, AIDS, advanced Alzheimer's, or cancer will deliver each of these dear followers of Jesus, in the words of Paul on the eve of his own martyrdom, "safely to [God's] heavenly kingdom" (2 Timothy 4:18). In the meantime, their lives are dominated by doctors' visits, medications, hospital stays, surgeries, discomfort, and pain. Their circumstances are not going to change; their trials are not going away. They have learned to wait. But they are not waiting for a clean bill of health. They are waiting on God.

Waiting is hard. But waiting on God is infinitely rewarding, for the reward of biblical waiting is the infinitely delightful self-disclosure of God Himself. My hope is that the concept of waiting on God will take on new significance for you as it has for me, that you will see it on every page of your Bible, and that you will reap its rewards in this age and in the one to come.

Waiting on God in a World that Won't Wait

We Live in an Instant World

You and I live in an instant world. We make instant coffee and instant breakfast. We watch instant replay. I have instant hot water in my kitchen and instant messaging on my computer. We have become accustomed to the rapid delivery of information and the instant fulfillment of desires.

Do you remember mail? We used to write letters with pens on dead trees and send them to each other. When William Carey went to India as a missionary, it could take six months for a letter to make it home to England and another six months for a reply to reach India. The Pony Express and the United States Postal Service sped up the delivery of mail dramatically in America. Express Mail, Air Mail, and Overnight Delivery are all available if you just can't wait a couple days for a letter to get from one place to another. Then someone invented email, eclipsing snail mail with speed-of-light delivery. Yet you still have to wait until some kind soul on the other end decides to turn on his computer, open up his email, fish your message out of the abyss of his overloaded in-box, and construct a reply.

We love instant information, instant gratification, and instant satisfaction. The candy bar's sales slogan is "Why wait? Grab a Snickers." Do not just eat a Snickers, but grab a Snickers. As you tear off the wrapper, you have a split-second to notice the promise of what lies waiting for you inside: Satisfaction. Why wait? Get it now! This is the world we live in. Transportation has changed our expectations. The distance Lewis and Clark covered in two years and two months can now be covered in about six hours. We live in the era of bullet trains, supersonic jets, and Wikipedia. We have fast food, fast cars, fast service, and microwave ovens. Someone needs to invent the reverse of the microwave oven—not something that will take a refrigerated item up to piping hot, but the reverse. I want a Cherry Coke that's 33 degrees Fahrenheit, and I want it now. If there is a way to accomplish this without the danger and expense of liquid nitrogen, I need one!

We love instant things. We hate waiting. The world around us is captivated and cultivated by instantaneous satisfaction. We want what we want and we want it now. If somebody cannot deliver it as fast as we want it, they have somehow violated our rights.

Christians Are Programmed to Wait

Although we live in an instant world, if you are a Christian, you have been designed by God to wait. Waiting is part of a Christian's DNA. In the Apostle Paul's first letter to the believers at Thessalonica, he gives an interesting description of what it means to be a follower of Jesus. He writes, "For they themselves report about us what kind of reception we had with you—how you turned to God from idols to serve a living and true God and to wait for a Son from heaven whom He raised from the dead, that is Jesus who rescues us from the wrath to come" (1 Thessalonians 1:9-10).

What was Paul's description of the Thessalonian believers and their conversion? They turned to God from idols *to serve* and *to wait, to serve* God and *to wait* for Jesus. A Christian, fundamentally, is one who has repented of idolatry. He has turned to God from those things which compete for the affections of his heart. Idolatry is the disease every one of us inherited from birth and the occupation from which we must turn. The repentance Paul describes in verse 9 is a purposeful repentance. The turning from idols to God has two inevitable results, granted by God in conversion: serving God and waiting for Jesus. Paul is giving the definition of a Christian as he describes the Thessalonians' conversion. Have you experienced genuine conversion? Have you turned to God from the idolatry of your former life? Is your new life characterized by the twin purposes of serving God and waiting for Jesus?

Paul whets the appetite with four descriptions of Jesus in verse 10: He is God's Son, He comes out of Heaven, He was raised from the dead, and He rescues from coming wrath. Jesus, the one for whom we wait, is first described as God's Son. He is none other than God Himself, the second person of the Trinity, the Son of the Eternal Father who came to earth once to die on behalf of those who would believe. He will come again to reign as King and to redeem those finally who belong to Him. This is God's Son, the one through whom God created everything. Nothing exists except what Jesus created and sustains (Colossians 1:16; Hebrews 1:2-3; John 1:1-3). This Son is the Creator of the universe, the baby born at Bethlehem, the Messiah anticipated by the Old Testament saints, and the returning King for whom New Testament saints wait now.

Secondly, Jesus comes out of Heaven. Jesus is not physically here now. He resides spiritually in the hearts of believers, and He, as God, is always present everywhere. But He has chosen to locate Himself physically in His resurrection body at the right hand of the Father in heaven. He is interceding on behalf of His followers. Jesus Himself waits to return to vindicate His own name, to establish His kingdom, to set all things right, and to redeem His children. He came from heaven, returned to heaven, and will come again from heaven.

Thirdly, God raised Jesus from the dead. This One for whom Christians wait is the One who conquered death. This is the God-man who walked out of a tomb and promised resurrection from the dead for all who believe in Him. Yet Christians must wait, amidst the ravages of death, for the one who conquered death forever on their behalf.

Fourthly, Jesus rescues us from the coming wrath. Infinite and unquenchable wrath is on its way. Every person who does not turn to the Son is presently "storing up wrath for [himself] in the day of wrath and revelation of the righteous judgment of God, who will render to each person according to his deeds" (Romans 2:5-6). Jesus is the Son who rescues us from the coming wrath by having come already to the cross and endured that wrath as a substitute in our place. This is the One for whom we wait.

Paul reminded the Thessalonian believers that they turned to God from idols. They turned in order to serve the living and true God, and they turned in order to wait for Jesus. They waited for God's Son out of Heaven, raised from the dead, the one who rescues us from the coming wrath. Like the Thessalonian Christians, we turned to wait. We were rescued and programmed by God to wait. By new birth, waiting is in our DNA.

God's People Wait

God's people have always waited. Two examples may be helpful to demonstrate that this has been the design for God's people throughout biblical history.

Listen first to the description of God's people given in Psalm 147:11: "Yahweh[2] favors those who fear Him, Those who wait for His lovingkindness." Two descriptions of God's people are given in poetic parallelism. The Old Testament believers were those who feared God and waited for His lovingkindness. Lovingkindness is the Old Testament word for grace. God is disposed in kindness toward sinners who fear Him, who align themselves in reverential awe toward Him, who cease running away from Him, and who turn to depend upon His grace. Repentant sinners fear God and wait on His grace.

Fear and waiting do not seem like good things to sinful people. Who likes fear? Who enjoys waiting? And yet, this is exactly the kind of response a right relationship to God demands. Normally things that terrify us are not endearing. We run away from terrifying things. Not so with God. The fear of God produces an irresistible magnetic pull towards God. The crazy reality is that the one born of God loves God. He sees this great, awesome, infinite, fearsome Being. Thus the fear that the creature has for God drives Him toward God for refuge to hear Him say, "Come to me and find rest and forgiveness and joy and peace and freedom from terror." That is the God we serve. Recognizing the sheer bigness of God, the believer responds in the only manner reasonable: he looks for grace. In Psalm 147, the Old Testament saint is defined as one waiting on God.

---

2   I will use God's personal name, Yahweh, to reflect the Hebrew. Many English versions of the Bible render the name Yahweh as "LORD." The significance of God's name will be explained further in Chapter 3.

A second example paints the same picture from the New Testament. Hebrews 9:28 gives this definition of a Christian: "those who eagerly wait for Him." In his letter to the Hebrews, the author wrote, "And inasmuch as it is appointed for men to die once and after this comes judgment, so Christ also, having been offered once to bear the sins of many, will appear a second time for salvation without reference to sin, to those who eagerly await Him" (Hebrews 9:27-28). Jesus came the first time to suffer the penalty of sin at the cross, and He is coming again, not with reference to sin, but with reference to a final salvation of Christians. But the writer doesn't use the word "Christian" to describe us here. Instead, he calls us "those who eagerly await Him." Do you see how God defines a believer here? He is the one who eagerly awaits Jesus. Christ comes for final redemption of Christians. Christ comes for final redemption for those who eagerly await Him.

Is that your heart? Does "eagerly waiting" define you? Is this your disposition toward God? Does this attitude describe your life? Old Testament believers feared and waited for Him; New Testament believers eagerly await Jesus' return.

I don't like waiting. I am not good at it. Waiting is hard. Waiting is a lost art in the Christian life. However, waiting on God ought to define us. You will find God's people waiting on almost every page of your Bible. It is the hardest thing in the world to do, and yet, it is most rewarding.

What Is Waiting?

If waiting is to be a fundamental disposition for the Christian, then we probably ought to find out what it means to wait. Christians are not like the citizens of this world, having all of our eggs in the basket of this temporal existence. The land of our pilgrimage is not our home, our hope, or our treasure. We have doubled down; we are all in for the next life. Everything that we have set aside on this earth, we have done so to gain an infinite treasure in the next life. The Christian has counted the cost, given up everything, and followed Christ. We wait for Jesus because with Him is everything.

The world around us is working very hard to squeeze something out of this temporal existence: satisfaction, joy, meaning, fulfillment, fun, or the essence of life. I have a lemon tree in my front yard. My wife, Janet, made unforgettable lemonade from some of the lemons on the lower branches. The lemons were sweet, tart, and exceptionally juicy. But one of the lemons came from an upper branch that had been damaged by frost last winter. The lemon was bright yellow, fragrant, and plump. I cut it in half and placed it on the juicer. Nothing came out. The freeze had destroyed the best part of the lemon, and all that remained were dried pulp and a bitter rind. The fruit's appearance promised sweet satisfaction, but it was a hollow claim.

The follower of Jesus recognizes that the world's promises of joy and fulfillment are empty. The world writes checks that its citizens can't cash. Purpose, joy, satisfaction, fulfillment, and ultimate things do not belong to this realm. They are in Jesus, and they are for those who eagerly wait on Him. We do not yet possess them and experience them in the way that we will when we have Jesus in His fullness. The world toils in vain to find them here. We wait.

The Christian life is a life of waiting in an impatient world. Consider the fact that God's people waited 4,000 years for Messiah to come the first time, and so far we have waited 2,000 years for Him to return. The Bible is a book about waiting, saturated with waiting language. We need to reacquaint ourselves with the forgotten vocabulary of waiting in the Scriptures.

What follows is a vocabulary list of "waiting" words, along with

Scripture passages that employ them. If you are not the type that reads the dictionary for fun, you may want to skim this section. I included this list because, first, I *do* read the dictionary for fun, and second, because the English word "wait" cannot adequately convey the breadth of meaning of the biblical concept of waiting. We need to see that waiting on God is much more than simply passing the time.

Old Testament "Waiting" Words

The English word "wait" primarily translates four words in the Hebrew Old Testament. The most common, קוה (*qawa*), means to wait under pressure with eager anticipation.

> Psalm 130:5–6
> I **wait** for Yahweh, my soul does **wait**,
> And in His word do I hope.
> My soul **waits** for the Lord
> More than the watchmen for the morning;
> Indeed, more than the watchmen for the morning.

A second Old Testament word for waiting, יחל (*yahal*), carries the idea of hope, of waiting with confident expectation in the promises and plan of God.

> Psalm 37:7
> Rest in Yahweh and **wait patiently** for Him;
> Do not fret because of him who prospers in his way,
> Because of the man who carries out wicked schemes.

The word חכה (*haka*) expresses a need, and an earnest expectation, of help.

Psalm 33:20
Our soul **waits** for Yahweh;
He is our help and our shield.

A final word, דמם (*damam*), means to grow silent or to be still.

Psalm 62:1,5
My soul **waits in silence** for God only;
From Him is my salvation.
My soul, **wait in silence** for God only,
For my hope is from Him.

New Testament "Waiting" Words

The New Testament writers enlist an even larger host of words to describe the believer's practice of waiting on God, and each of these words carries a slightly different flavor.

Following the resurrection, Jesus told His disciples not to hurry off to complete the Great Commission, but to wait (περιμένω, *perimeno*) for the Holy Spirit, without whose power and presence they had no hope of carrying out the expansion of the Gospel.

Acts 1:4
Gathering them together, He commanded them not to leave Jerusalem, but **to wait** for what the Father had promised, "Which," He said, "you heard of from Me."

Joseph of Arimathea waited for the kingdom with eager expectation (προσδέχομαι, *prosdechomai*).

Mark 15:43
Joseph of Arimathea came, a prominent member of the Council, who himself was **waiting** for the kingdom of God; and he

gathered up courage and went in before Pilate, and asked for the body of Jesus.

Similarly, the creation itself eagerly awaits (ἀπεκδέχομαι, *apekdechomai*) the culmination of God's redemptive plan.

Romans 8:19
For the anxious longing of the creation **waits eagerly** for the revealing of the sons of God.

The created universe anxiously longs (ἀποκαραδοκία, *apokaradokia*) under the curse of God for its consummation, when God's people will be fully redeemed from their slavery to corruption. Creation itself is personified as a long-necked animal peering around the corner of future history, longing for its own liberation which must wait for God to finish His work with a redeemed humanity.

Romans 8:19
For the **anxious longing** of the creation waits eagerly for the revealing of the sons of God.

Believers are said to live in expectation (ἀναμένω, *anameno*) of Jesus' return.

1 Thessalonians 1:10
and **to wait** for His Son from heaven, whom He raised from the dead, that is Jesus, who rescues us from the wrath to come.

Waiting often involves the enduring of hardship over time. Abraham waited with longsuffering endurance (μακροθυμέω, *makrothumeo*).

Hebrews 6:15
And so, **having patiently waited**, he obtained the promise.

Jesus sets a perfect example for His people, waiting with patience for a future event (ἐκδέχομαι, *ekdechomai*).

> Hebrews 10:12–13
> But He, having offered one sacrifice for sins for all time, sat down at the right hand of God, **waiting** from that time onward until His enemies be made a footstool for His feet.

Believers bear up under hardships (ὑπομένω, *hupomeno*), knowing that God will ultimately set all things right.

> 2 Corinthians 1:6
> But if we are afflicted, it is for your comfort and salvation; or if we are comforted, it is for your comfort, which is effective in the **patient enduring** of the same sufferings which we also suffer.

> Matthew 10:22
> "You will be hated by all because of My name, but it is the one who has **endured** to the end who will be saved."

Believers also bear up under harsh treatment (ἀνεξίκακος, *anexikakos*) from others, with patience, and without bitterness or resentment.

> 2 Timothy 2:24
> The Lord's bond-servant must not be quarrelsome, but be kind to all, able to teach, **patient** when wronged.

Christians are also instructed to bear up (ὑποφέρω,) under temptations. Waiting on God is an often-overlooked but critical weapon in our fight against sin. Paul does not make a promise that God will take away all of our temptations, but that we will be equipped by God to endure them.

1 Corinthians 10:13
No temptation has overtaken you but such as is common to man; and God is faithful, who will not allow you to be tempted beyond what you are able, but with the temptation will provide the way of escape also, so that you will be able to **endure** it.

God Himself waits, patiently enduring ($\phi\acute{\epsilon}\rho\omega$, *fero*), or bearing the burden of, the sins of His creatures. Moses experienced the difficulty of bearing with an obstinate people (Numbers 11:14), the Servant of Yahweh bore the sins of the people (Isaiah 53:4), and with great longsuffering God bears with those who will be objects of his wrath. In this instance, God is the One who waits.

Romans 9:22
What if God, although willing to demonstrate His wrath and to make His power known, **endured** with much patience vessels of wrath prepared for destruction?

Paul set an example for Christians to undergo troublesome circumstances without giving in or giving up ($\mathring{\alpha}\nu\acute{\epsilon}\chi o\mu\alpha\iota$, *anechomai*).

1 Corinthians 4:12
and we toil, working with our own hands; when we are reviled, we bless; when we are persecuted, we **endure**;

2 Thessalonians 1:4
therefore, we ourselves speak proudly of you among the churches of God for your perseverance and faith in the midst of all your persecutions and afflictions which you **endure**.

Paul also knew how to hold up in difficulties (στέγω, stego), to bear or put up with hardship, for the sake of others.

1 Corinthians 9:12
If others share the right over you, do we not more? Nevertheless, we did not use this right, but we **endure** all things so that we will cause no hindrance to the gospel of Christ.

Timothy was instructed to **endure** what is bad (κακοποθέω, kakopotheo), not to be overcome by affliction and adversity, but to endure them.

2 Timothy 4:5
But you, be sober in all things, **endure hardship**, do the work of an evangelist, fulfill your ministry.

The author of Hebrews described Moses' waiting as being mistreated with others (συγκακουχέομαι, sugkakoucheomai)

Hebrews 11:25
choosing rather to **endure ill-treatment** with the people of God than to enjoy the passing pleasures of sin.

Moses exercised a trust in something he couldn't see, producing a willingness to endure what was difficult (καρτερέω, kartereo). Faith in God made this kind of endurance possible.

Hebrews 11:27
By faith he left Egypt, not fearing the wrath of the king; for he **endured**, as seeing Him who is unseen.

Essential to waiting is the element of yet-unfulfilled desire. Longing (ἐπιποθέω, *epipotheo*) implies waiting for what you do not yet have. The Christian's longing is a strong desire for what he does not yet possess.

> 2 Corinthians 5:2
> For indeed in this house we groan, **longing** to be clothed with our dwelling from heaven.

Hope (ἐλπίζω / ἐλπις, *elpidzo / elpis*), as a noun and a verb, is an important "waiting" word in the Bible. Biblical hope is a confident expectation of good and is closely linked with trust, specifically, trust in God's person, His power, His promises, and His purpose on behalf of His people. It is directed toward God as it waits quietly for God, patiently embracing the expectation of a good and certain future. Hope is a confident, eager waiting for God and for the yet-unexperienced future which God has decreed.

Biblical hope is not to be confused with wishful thinking, as in, "I hope there's a short line at lunch today," or "I hope the weather cooperates with our camping trip." Hope in the promises of God is a rock-solid confidence in future history. Notice the use of the word "hope" in your New Testament, keeping an eye on what is hoped for, and who has grounds for hope. Only believers in Jesus Christ have grounds for hope. And this hope is for good, every single time. Yet hope implies waiting, because the fulfillment of the hope is not yet realized. We see this in the following examples:

> Romans 5:2
> through whom also we have obtained our introduction by faith into this grace in which we stand; and we exult in **hope** of the glory of God.

Romans 8:25
But if we **hope** for what we do not see, with perseverance we wait eagerly for it.

Hebrews 6:19
This **hope** we have as an anchor of the soul, a **hope** both sure and steadfast and one which enters within the veil.

One could continue this vocabulary list with related words and ideas such as faith, trust, resting, steadfastness, suffering, and tolerating. These words and ideas all have in common an element of time. These are attitudes of confident waiting on God when my circumstances (for now) are unpleasant and unchanging. One could also investigate the future tense verbs in the Bible. Many verbs in future tense indicate promises from God about what is to come. These are certain realities guaranteed by God but not yet possessed by God's people. (See, for example, 1 Timothy 6:14-15.)

The idea of waiting is a foreign concept to the instant world in which we live. Christians have been designed by God to wait, and so the Christian life is an existence defined by waiting. A watching world must surely be puzzled at the way we live, for our hopes are not realized here. Not attempting to find life in temporal enjoyments, you and I are willing, in the words of Martin Luther, to "let goods and kindred go, this mortal life also. The body they may kill, God's truth abideth still. His kingdom is forever!" And it is for His kingdom we work and we wait. That is what the Christian life is.

What Are We Waiting For?

So what are we waiting for? We wait for resolution from conflict. We wait for vindication of wrongs. We wait for justice to be done. We wait for world peace. We wait for a kingdom. We wait for things that don't rust and aren't stolen. Some of us wait eagerly for new bodies. We wait for the end of sin. We wait until death is no more, sorrow is no more, and pain is no more. We wait until those old things pass, giving way to a new heaven, a new earth, and a new way of things.

But more than all of these things, the people of God in the Bible waited for God. If you wait for Him, all these things shall be added to you. He is our treasure. He is the One for whom we wait. He is the One we eagerly expect. He is the One we long for. Christian, if your heart is not set on Him, you will be tossed around by your circumstances. You will be fearful about the future. You will wonder what lies ahead, and you will fret about what is coming because you cannot control it. However, if you wait for Him, your circumstances may never change, but your heart will. If you wait for Him, your difficulties in this life might not go away. That is not the promise of Jesus. He said sufferings will come, crosses will be borne, the world will hate you, your parents may disown you, but you will have everything because you have God. That is the promise of Jesus. If you set your heart on Him, you set your heart on the One who is the source of all joy. He is the fountain of life. Everything that brings happiness in this temporal existence, everything that brings joy or puts a smile on your face is an appetizer, a hint, a shadow, a foretaste of the true Source of joy. The Source is someone else. God. The fountain of all good things. And God promises Himself for those who wait for Him.

Are you waiting on God? Have you discovered the lost art of the Christian life?

The History
of Waiting

Among the worst words that can be heard: "Take a number and have a seat." A screen up front broadcasts, "Now serving number 4." You fiddle with the ticket in your hand labeled #127, crunching the numbers and estimating the hours of your plight. You will be waiting. The Arizona Motor Vehicle Division is a particularly discouraging place to wait. The last time I was there, I was dealt D17. D17 resembles a number, but there is a letter in there too, and it is really confusing because you look up on the screen, and the customers to be served next are M47, H86, and Q99. I don't know where D17 fits in that progression. Am I supposed to feel better or just confused enough to not complain? I want to meet the wizard in charge of assigning those numbers and those letters. I am certain he has beady eyes and scraggly hair, seated at a monitor in a back room, eager to see how people respond to the numbers he deals. "I'm gonna give this guy D17, look at that! There's not a D on the monitors. How's he gonna figure this one out?"

The truth is that God is in charge of D17. God is in charge of the number you are assigned at the Motor Vehicle Division and the number you receive at In-N-Out Burger. He is in charge of every circumstance. Everybody waits. This book is about waiting on God. It is about trusting Him when your circumstances are hard. It is about clinging to God when your situation refuses to change. It is about longing for heaven and loving Jesus. God is the One who is in charge of all of the details of life. Every circumstance that causes us to wait is in the hand of the One orchestrating all of history. Who is in charge of the traffic lights? Who is in charge of the line at the grocery store?

There is not a single event, not a single person, not a single object in the universe that is out of step with the perfect plan and the perfect timing of our sovereign God. Every circumstance is orchestrated by the Creator and the Sustainer of the universe. That means when I complain about my circumstances, I am complaining about God's operation of the universe. In effect, I'm telling God that He is not running things right, that He needs to bring my circumstances into conformity to my plan. I know better than God. Maybe I should be the one on that throne.

Waiting on God, in part, is the opposite of complaining. It is embracing my circumstances as coming from God. It is to accept my circumstances without becoming suspicious about God's character, His ability, or His intentions. To wait on God is to trust Him when my circumstances do not change, to trust His goodness, His power, His promises, and His purposes.

Everybody waits. Not everybody waits well, and not everybody waits on God. Much of God's good work in our lives will be accomplished only in difficult circumstances that force us to wait on Him. As hard as waiting is, it is also rewarding, because waiting on God well brings us to Him. The reward of waiting is not the promise of a changed circumstance; it is not the promise of a better life now. The reward of waiting is the promise of God Himself, and that is better than anything we can conceive.

My idolatrous heart is revealed when I desire a change in my circumstances more than I want God. Therefore, a situation in which I am forced to wait is a revealing situation. How I wait displays the priority of my affections. Do I love ease, comfort, and temporal happiness more than what God has for me in His perfect plan?

Waiting on God is a well-worn practice with a storied history. When I am forced to wait, I tend to believe that I am the first person who has ever had to wait, or that I am the only person who is waiting now. Nobody can understand my plight. No one's experience compares to mine. Some historical perspective is helpful here. When you and I wait on God, we are not alone. In fact, we are in good company. The halls of history are lined with saints who have gone before us, clinging to God when circumstances would not change.

Old Testament Saints Waited

Adam Waited

Adam was the first man to wait on God. His waiting is detailed in Genesis chapter 2:

> Then Yahweh God said, 'It is not good for the man to be alone; I will make him a helper suitable for him.' Out of the ground Yahweh God formed every beast of the field and every bird of the sky, and brought them to the man to see what he would call them; and whatever the man called a living creature, that was its name (Genesis 2:18-19).

Did you notice, in verse 19, that Adam is already waiting? God said, "I'm going to give you a helper. Here's an aardvark, and a cardinal, and a butterfly, and a giraffe, and a triceratops." The suitable helper doesn't appear anywhere in this long line of yet-unnamed creatures.

> The man gave names to all the cattle, and to the birds of the sky, and to every beast of the field, but for Adam there was not found a helper suitable for him. So Yahweh God caused a deep sleep to fall upon the man, and he slept; then He took one of his ribs and closed up the flesh at that place. Yahweh God fashioned into a woman the rib which He had taken from the man, and brought her to the man. The man said,

> > 'This is now bone of my bones,
> > And flesh of my flesh;
> > She shall be called Woman,
> > Because she was taken out of Man' (Genesis 2:20-23).

Did you notice the word "now"? After a long line of creatures, Adam says "Now, this is a suitable helper! Finally! This is right!" In response, Adam sings the first love song, and rejoices in the provision of God: "Bone of my bones and flesh of my flesh—Woman!" Before there was sin, while the world was still perfect, Adam waited on God.

Job Waited

The book of Job is a waiting-on-God wrestling match. At times, Job exercises remarkable faith by waiting on God in the midst of awful circumstances. At other times Job questions God, distrusts God, and impugns God's character. And Job's trouble is not the only storyline in the book. There is another plot with other characters. The book of Job is about Satan's attempt to discredit God, His power, and His ability to finish the work that He began in a man. Most of the book records the heart-level wrestling match between Job's theology and his perception of his circumstances. His so-called friends join the fray, filling in the divine silence with their own ignorant musings. Job's emotional tug-of-war can be seen in the progression of the book.

Disasters strike Job in rapid succession. His oxen, his donkeys, and his servants are destroyed by Sabean bandits. Sheep and more servants are killed by fire from the sky. Camels and still more servants are defeated by the Chaldeans. Finally, a wind storm takes the lives of his children while they were celebrating. You and I sit with Job in the rubble of what was a very extravagant life and ask, "Why?" Job's first response is fantastic. We find it in the first chapter.

"Then Job arose and tore his robe and shaved his head, and he fell to the ground and worshiped. He said, 'Naked I came from my mother's womb, And naked I shall return there. Yahweh gave and Yahweh has taken away. Blessed be the name of Yahweh'" (Job 1:20-21).

In the face of crushing comments from his wife, Job's second response is also surprisingly godly. "He said to her, 'You speak as one of the foolish women speaks. Shall we indeed accept good from God and not accept adversity?' In all this Job did not sin with his lips" (Job 2:10).

Remarkably, Job's first responses to hardship were to trust, to worship, and to wait on God. I would love for my first response to hardship to resemble Job's. His later response is much easier for me to comprehend. In chapter 10, Job begins to complain. "I loathe my own life; I will give full vent to my complaint; I will speak in the bitterness of my soul. I will say to God, 'Do not condemn me; Let me know why You contend with me. Is it right for You indeed to oppress, To reject the labor of Your hands, And to look favorably on the schemes of the wicked? Have You eyes of flesh? Or do You see as a man sees?'" (Job 10:1–4)

By chapter 13, Job returns to his first response: hope and trust in God.

"Though He slay me, I will hope in Him. Nevertheless I will argue my ways before Him" (Job 13:15). Job's heart-battle continues in chapter 17, where we discover Job despairing over his circumstances. "My spirit is broken, my days are extinguished, The grave is ready for me" (Job 17:1). Job expresses hope, waiting, and trusting in chapter 19. "As for me, I know that my Redeemer lives, And at the last He will take His stand on the earth. Even after my skin is destroyed, Yet from my flesh I shall see God" (Job 19:25–26). A mixture of complaint and seeking God are on display in chapter 23. "Even today my complaint is rebellion; His hand is heavy despite my groaning. Oh that I knew where I might find Him, That I might come to His seat!" (Job 23:2–3). Job's friend, Elihu, speaks up in chapter 35, with the right message: "The case is before Him, and you must wait for Him!" (Job 35:14).

Finally, in chapter 38, the waiting is over. God speaks. The story takes a dramatic turn when God opens His mouth. Like Job, we have a hard time waiting in silence. We flounder and scramble and fret and question and doubt when we haven't heard from God in the midst of difficult circumstances. (There is a lesson here about regular, disciplined intake of God's Word. We do not do well for very long when we separate ourselves from the voice of God.) But everything is okay when God speaks. We know that God is God and we are not. From this point forward we know that Job will be alright; our safety is in the knowledge that God is God. I am not God. You are not God. We must trust Him.

"Then Job answered Yahweh and said, 'I know that You can do all things, And that no purpose of Yours can be thwarted. Who is this that hides counsel without knowledge? Therefore I have declared that which I did not understand, Things too wonderful for me, which I did not know. 'Hear, now, and I will speak; I will ask You, and You instruct me. I have heard of You by the hearing of the ear; But now my eye sees You; Therefore I retract, And I repent in dust and ashes" (Job 42:1–6).

Job is comforted by God's presence and voice, but we have to wait until the end of the book to find out why all of this happened. During the days of his trial, Job was not able to see what was going on behind the scenes. Poor Job is in the crosshairs of a cosmic battle between God and Satan, and he does not know it. Why was he attacked by bandits and armies and fire from the sky and a great wind? Why are his children dead? Why is his wife such a burden? Why don't his friends help? Why are all his belongings gone? And why must he endure this great physical suffering? Why has everything been taken from him? Why? Why? Why?

The answers do not come until Job 42:18. Why has all of this happened? If you are checking your Bible, you know there is no Job 42:18! Job never had the privilege of discovering the answer to the "why" question. In the whole course of his lifetime, Job was left simply to trust God and to wait on Him. This is what makes waiting so hard. We want the "why" answered. Job never got the "why" answered. Job was not perfect, but he was patient.

Abraham Waited

"And I will make you a great nation, And I will bless you, And make your name great; And so you shall be a blessing; And I will bless those who bless you, And the one who curses you I will curse. And in you all the families of the earth will be blessed" (Genesis 12:2–3). That is an extravagant promise. Abraham, who has no kids, is going to be the father of many nations. He will have descendants that cannot be counted. He will have a land and a people, and these will be a blessing to people of all nations. God gives this promise to a father without a son.

The scene in Genesis 16 is only four chapters away, but it is ten years later. Ten years! Can you imagine getting a promise from God, looking at your watch, marking off the days on the calendar, marking off the months, and the years, and a decade? "Now Sarai, Abram's wife had borne him no children, and she had an Egyptian maid whose name was Hagar. So Sarai said to Abram, 'Now behold, Yahweh has prevented me from bearing children. Please go in to my maid; perhaps I will obtain children through her.' And Abram listened to the voice of Sarai" (Genesis 16:1–2).

Abraham didn't wait. Like Job, Abraham experienced the heart-level wrestling match of trusting God over time when circumstances were hard and doubt crept in. Abraham was 86 years old when Ishmael, the son of Sarah's maid, was born. However, God came through on His promise of a son born by Sarah when Abraham was 99. "I will bless her, and indeed I will give you a son by her. Then I will bless her, and she shall be a mother of nations; kings of peoples will come from her" (Genesis 17:16). Abraham waited 13 more years for the fulfillment of God's promise, and God credited Abraham's waiting as righteousness.

Joseph Waited

Joseph did a lot of waiting. He waited in the hole where his brothers tossed him, he waited in Egyptian slavery, and he waited in jail for a crime he did not commit. The king's baker and cupbearer, also imprisoned, knew about Joseph's plight, but the baker got the noose, the cup bearer forgot, and Joseph languished for two years. Two years! "Now it happened at the end of two full years that Pharaoh had a dream" (Genesis 41:1). Joseph was sprung only when the king's cupbearer finally remembered that Joseph could interpret dreams. Why is this happening?

Joseph received what Job didn't: an answer to the "why" question. He spoke it to his brothers in Genesis 50:20, "You meant evil against me, but God meant it for good in order to bring about this present result, to preserve many people alive." God was doing something big that Joseph had to wait for. God's fledgling nation Israel, whose entire population was 72 people, were to be incubated under the protective shelter of Egypt, the superpower of the day, and to emerge 400 years later with 1.2 million. Intending to preserve Israel, as well as Egypt, from starvation and destruction, God was up to something bigger yet—insuring the coming of His promised Messiah so that you and I could have our sins forgiven. God was up to something, and His people waited.

Israel Waited

For four hundred years God's people waited in Egypt, much of it in slavery. Moses had to wait 40 years as a shepherd in Midian before leading God's people out of Egypt. And then the nation of Israel waited through forty more years of wasteland wandering. "For Yahweh your God has blessed you in all that you have done; He has known your wanderings through this great wilderness. These forty years Yahweh your God has been with you; you have not lacked a thing" (Deuteronomy 2:7). What were they waiting for? We find out later in the same chapter, "Now the time that it took for us to come from Kadesh-barnea until we crossed over the brook Zered was thirty-eight years, until all the generation of the men of war perished from within the camp, as Yahweh had sworn to them. Moreover the hand of Yahweh was against them, to destroy them from within the camp until they all perished" (Deuteronomy 2:14-15). What were they waiting for? They were waiting for that first generation to die off! God had promised that the first generation of escapees from Egypt would not enter the Promised Land because of their unbelief and rebellion. Can you imagine being one of the men of the first generation thinking, "These people can't enter the promised land until I die?" And can you imagine the younger generation standing around muttering, "When is that guy gonna give up the ghost? I mean, we can't go into the Promised Land until all these guys are gone." They had to wait. "So it came about when all the men of war had finally perished from among the people, that Yahweh spoke to me, saying, 'Today you shall cross over Ar, the border of Moab'" (Deuteronomy 2:16-18). The Israelites waited.

Saul Did Not Wait

Saul was Israel's second king. God was Israel's first King. But envious of the surrounding nations who had a visible human king to lead their battles, they rejected the pure theocracy, and Saul was chosen. In I Samuel 13, Saul was told to wait for Samuel. Samuel was to offer sacrifice to Yahweh before Saul went into the battle against the Philistines. As the Philistine army drew near, Saul got scared, and he took the priestly duty of sacrifice into his own hands.

This disobedient lack of trust in God took place probably two years into Saul's reign. As God pronounced judgment on Saul, He also made a promise to the nation. He would provide Israel with a new king, a man after God's own heart. Now this is interesting: Saul didn't wait, but now God's people must wait. Saul ruled for forty years (Acts 13:21). David waited for decades between his anointing and coronation as Israel's king. And Israel waited for a King who followed God perfectly. Eventually the people were ruled by a man whom God referred to as a man after His own heart. But David was a flawed foreshadowing of a King who was still to come. And even today the nation of Israel awaits her King that will rule completely and totally after God's own heart.

38

Jeremiah Waited

Jeremiah preached for forty years to a people who did not listen. Jeremiah labored and suffered through forty years of ministry with no "results." Nobody repented. Nobody listened to him, except for one Gentile from way out of town, Ebed-melech, the Ethiopian who rescued him from the cistern in which he had been tossed (Jeremiah 38:7-13).

Daniel Waited

"In the first year of his [Darius, King of the Chaldeans] reign, I, Daniel, observed in the books the number of the years which was revealed as the word of Yahweh to Jeremiah the prophet for the completion of the desolations of Jerusalem, namely, seventy years" (Daniel 9:2). Daniel waited for seventy years as a hostage in Babylon.

Generations of God's People Waited

Old Testament history is, in fact, a history of waiting. From the fall of Adam and Eve, mankind has been waiting for God to reverse the curse and reopen the way to paradise. God made a promise to the serpent in the immediate aftermath of that ancient snake's treason, "I will put enmity between you and the woman, and between your seed and her seed; he shall bruise you on the head, and you shall bruise him on the heel" (Genesis 3:15). Trace the fulfillment of that promise as you read your Bible from left to right. A descendant of Eve was supposed to crush the head of the snake, and every successive generation would bring hope that One would be born who would fulfill God's promise. Could it be Cain, Seth, Noah, Abraham, Moses, David, Solomon? Generation after generation would see hopes dashed as the children of Eve failed and floundered. The snake-head-smasher must still be coming. For four thousand years, God's people waited for Messiah.

Old Testament history ground to a disappointing halt with 400 "silent" years. From the time of Malachi, the last Old Testament prophet, to the time of the events recorded by Matthew in the New Testament, there was no word from God and no Messiah. The nation of Israel had been divided and conquered. Some had trickled back into their land from captivity, and the nation had been under the thumb of the Persians, the Greeks, and finally the Romans. To this point Israel had never yet possessed fully the land that God promised. And since the exile into captivity Israel had never even been a sovereign nation. By the time of the New Testament the people of Israel exercised a limited self-rule under the governance of the Roman Empire.

Where is the promised land? Where is our king? Where is this Anointed One? This Promised One? This hoped-for One? Where is Messiah? Where is God's blessing? The nation waited. And the waiting continued into the New Testament.

New Testament Saints Waited

The New Testament is in many ways a record of fulfillment of the anticipation of the Old Testament, yet it is also a record of the waiting of God's people. Elizabeth and Zacharias waited, along with many godly couples in Biblical history, for a baby (Luke 1:68–79). Their son, John the Baptist, was a man who didn't have to wait much longer for the One who would come.

Simeon was a man who waited for the "consolation of Israel" (Luke 2:25). He was told by the Holy Spirit that he would not die until he saw Messiah. When Jesus was presented at the temple, Simeon held the Creator of the universe in his arms. The wait for Messiah was over. He rejoiced, "For my eyes have seen Your salvation, Which You have prepared in the presence of all peoples, A Light of revelation to the Gentiles, And the glory of Your people Israel" (Luke 2:30-32).

In the same chapter, a godly woman named Anna was also waiting. "She was advanced in years and had lived with her husband seven years after her marriage, and then as a widow to the age of eighty-four. She never left the temple, serving night and day with fastings and prayers." On the day that she met the baby Messiah, she "began giving thanks to God, and continued to speak of Him to all those who were looking for the redemption of Jerusalem" (Luke 2:36–38). As a widow for most of her earthly existence, she waited on God by serving in the temple, praying and fasting. Her waiting was rewarded with the arrival of God Himself!

Jesus' earthly ministry was marked by people waiting for His healing touch. A father's heart ached for years as he watched his son suffer from demonic oppression (Mark 9:20-22). A woman waited eighteen years bent in half by a demon (Luke 13:10-17). A lame man endured his condition for 38 years before Jesus healed him (John 5:1-9). A hemorrhaging woman, considered unclean because of her condition, waited 12 years for Jesus to restore her (Matthew 9:20-22); and He gave her better access to God than she had ever missed by being excluded from the temple on account of her bleeding! Crowds of diseased, disabled, and demonized sufferers thronged to Jesus for relief from their long-endured misery.

Their waiting was rewarded by the personal touch of God, and the timing was perfect. Jesus' credentials were established, the religious leaders were incensed, and the long awaited Messiah was on His way to His own death.

The Disciples Waited

After Jesus' crucifixion and resurrection, the disciples again had to wait. "Gathering them together, He commanded them not to leave Jerusalem, but to wait for what the Father had promised, 'Which,' He said, 'you heard of from Me'" (Acts 1:4). What was it that Jesus promised to them? "And behold, I am sending forth the promise of My Father upon you; but you are to stay in the city until you are clothed with power from on high" (Luke 24:49).

Imagine what it would have been like to be a witness to Jesus' life and ministry, and then to see Him crucified and buried. He was dead. What would it have been like to see Him walking around again, alive?! Imagine being a witness to an empty tomb and resurrected Savior! The Messiah! The Promised One! Without a doubt, He is the One who can forgive sins, the One who has power over death! Sheer adrenaline would make you bold. And yet, Jesus told them to wait.

Something more than adrenaline, something more than just the natural excitement of the resurrection, was going to be needed for the progress of the gospel. They needed supernatural power. If the gospel was going to go forward, it would only do so by the power of the Holy Spirit in transformed men who were armed and ready to take the gospel at all costs to every nation, tongue, tribe, and people. Twenty centuries of believers all over the planet are the fruit of what they waited for!

Paul Waited

"At the same time too, he was hoping that money would be given him by Paul; therefore he also used to send for him quite often and converse with him. But after two years had passed, Felix was succeeded by Porcius Festus, and wishing to do the Jews a favor, Felix left Paul imprisoned" (Acts 24:26–27). Why was Paul in jail? Because a politician thought Paul was entertaining, and he hoped for a bribe. I would hope, if I ever went to jail, that it would be for the gospel. And, if boldness for the gospel resulted in imprisonment (hopefully a short imprisonment with good food and easy treatment), I'd sing songs and tell my captors about Jesus. Wouldn't that be great? You don't always get to pick your imprisonments. Paul didn't. Did you notice the duration of Paul's jail term in verse 27—"After two years had passed"? Paul was imprisoned numerous times, and this "little" stint gets a two-verse mention. After two years had passed, the rulers changed and Paul was still there.

Paul knew how to wait. In 2 Corinthians 5:2, Paul says, "Indeed in this house we groan, longing to be clothed with our dwelling from heaven." You see, Paul waited not just when he was in prison, but when he was free and doing ministry, and at liberty to go wherever he wanted to go. He was still a waiting man. Why? Because he had an eternal perspective, and he longed to be home with Jesus. "For to me, to live is Christ and to die is gain. But if I am to live on in the flesh, this will mean fruitful labor for me; and I do not know which to choose. But I am hard-pressed from both directions, having the desire to depart and be with Christ, for that is very much better; yet to remain on in the flesh is more necessary for your sake" (Philippians 1:21–24).

Paul waited. But you can tell from the way that Paul waited for Jesus that waiting was not simply doing nothing. "For this reason I endure all things for the sake of those who are chosen, so that they also may obtain the salvation which is in Christ Jesus and with it eternal glory" (2 Timothy 2:10). This is a strange statement, for despite the fact that God's salvation of His people was marked out in eternity past, Paul willingly endured unbelievable hardship so that they might believe. Paul's waiting on God was a labor of persevering faith for the eternal benefit of others.

Since the time of the New Testament, nearly 2000 years have elapsed, and we wait. God's people still wait. Human history is approaching 6000 years of waiting. There are some, yet to come, who still will wait.

Creation Waits

In Chapter 1, we glanced at the "waiting" words in Romans 8:19-21, where Paul personifies the created order: "For the anxious longing of the creation waits eagerly for the revealing of the sons of God. For the creation was subjected to futility, not willingly, but because of Him who subjected it, in hope that the creation itself also will be set free from its slavery to corruption into the freedom of the glory of the children of God." Straining its neck to peer around the corner of future history, creation "waits eagerly" for the culmination of its purpose. This temporary frustration of the universe is reflected in Solomon's words: "Consider the work of God, for who is able to straighten what He has bent?" (Ecclesiastes 7:13). Creation will not be set free from the Divine curse until God's redemption of His image-bearers is complete. Creation will be free when God's children look like Jesus, so creation awaits eagerly the day of our liberation. For now, creation is subjected to futility in the hope of that day.

Believers Throughout Church History Have Waited

The early church waited under persecution. The first several generations of Christians endured wave after wave of persecution from families, countrymen, employers, and governments. It wasn't until the edict of Milan in 313 that the government made it illegal to kill Christians for their faith. Prior to this edict, Christians were allowed to be killed, and often they were hunted down.

After government-sanctioned persecution ended, it did not take very long for the church to become a massive and corrupt organization. Genuine followers of Jesus waited over a thousand years for the Protestant Reformation. The true church lay hidden beneath a corrupt "church" that actually hid the Bible and the life-giving gospel from the people. The church waited for men like John Huss, John Wycliffe, and Martin Luther.

Nearly 2000 years have gone by so far, and you and I still wait for Jesus' return. Can you imagine the first century believers looking up in the clouds after Jesus ascended into heaven in Acts 1? They were told then, "He'll come back the same way." There is a sense in which we still gaze, we still look. Could it be today? Could this be the day that He returns? And we still wait.

Unreached Peoples Wait

There are people on the earth today without access to the gospel, people with no Bible in their language, people without the church at all in their culture. And they wait. On my desk in my office I keep a note from a man from a tribe in a mountainous region of Papua New Guinea. He is a member of the Ndo people, one of more than 100 tribes of people in the Finisterre Mountains with no gospel witness. Each of these tribes speaks a different language, isolated from each other and from the outside world by forbidding terrain and a rain-soaked jungle canopy. It seems likely that the last time any of these peoples heard directly from God was in Genesis 11:9, when God scattered them from the tower of Babel. The note on my desk was written in Pidgin (a trade language used in Papua New Guinea) to a missionary friend of mine working in the region. The Ndo man wrote, "I'm happy to come talk to you guys. We talked about sending a missionary to come to us, but you have not done it! And so we are still waiting." The Ndo people are not the only people waiting for the gospel to reach the ends of the earth.[3]

---

3 If you would like more information on how to participate in seeing the gospel go to unreached tribes of people in the Finisterre Mountains of Papua, New Guinea, visit gbcaz.org/pngmissions or finisterrevision.org.

The Dead in Christ Wait

But we do not want you to be uninformed, brethren, about those who are asleep, so that you will not grieve as do the rest who have no hope. For if we believe that Jesus died and rose again, even so God will bring with Him those who have fallen asleep in Jesus. For this we say to you by the word of the Lord, that we who are alive and remain until the coming of the Lord, will not precede those who have fallen asleep. For the Lord Himself will descend from heaven with a shout, with the voice of the archangel and with the trumpet of God, and the dead in Christ will rise first. Then we who are alive and remain will be caught up together with them in the clouds to meet the Lord in the air, and so we shall always be with the Lord. Therefore comfort one another with these words (1 Thessalonians 4:13–18).

Now I say this, brethren, that flesh and blood cannot inherit the kingdom of God; nor does the perishable inherit the imperishable. Behold, I tell you a mystery; we will not all sleep, but we will all be changed, in a moment, in the twinkling of an eye, at the last trumpet; for the trumpet will sound, and the dead will be raised imperishable, and we will be changed" (1 Corinthians 15:50–52).

The dead in Christ wait for the resurrection of the dead. They are currently "absent from the body" but "present with the Lord" (2 Corinthians 5:8). Humans were designed by God to be a union between body and spirit. You were designed to be material and immaterial, joined together in one person. At the resurrection event, those who have died in Christ will rise first, and then those who are alive will meet the Lord together and be with Him in the air. Until then, those who die in Jesus must wait for resurrection bodies.

Being in the presence of Jesus without a physical body, with no more sin and no more struggle, having entered eternal rest at home with Him, is something every believer should joyfully anticipate (Philippians 1:23). That state, even without a physical body, is better than this one. And yet, there is more to look forward to even than this. Even in heaven there is waiting. The dead in Christ wait for the resurrection, when their immaterial selves will be joined to a glorious, material resurrection body, a body no longer subject to corruption, decay, or disease. This new state will reflect Jesus and bring glory to the triune God! For this the dead in Christ wait still.

Tribulation Martyrs Will Wait

Before Jesus returns to the earth to reign as King, there will be a tribulation like the world has never seen: seven years of the wrath of God poured out on mankind. The earth will be run by a usurper, a counterfeit, a man who thinks he is Jesus. He will be backed by Satan— the god of this world. And the seven years of that tribulation period will be the worst the world has known. There will be many who come to faith in Jesus during that time, and many of them will be killed. Revelation 6:10-11 records their plea, "'How long, O Lord, holy and true, will You refrain from judging and avenging our blood on those who dwell on the earth?' And there was given to each of them a white robe; and they were told that they should rest for a little while longer, until the number of their fellow servants and their brethren who were to be killed even as they had been, would be completed also."

What will they be waiting for? More martyrs. What will they long for? The vindication of God's honor, the outpouring of God's wrath, and the executing of God's justice on the evil earth-dwellers. They wait.

God's People in the Millennial Kingdom Will Wait

Even in the Millennial Kingdom, God's people will wait. When the kingdom comes, the promises of God to Abraham and David will be met in the reign of Messiah on the earth. The Old Testament prophecies of world peace will find their fulfillment. The nations will beat their swords into plowshares, animal predation will cease, and the peoples will stream to Jerusalem to give tribute to Jesus. Jesus Himself will sit on David's throne in Jerusalem and rule the nations with a rod of iron. His enemies will be made a footstool for his feet. Even then, God's people will wait. Why? Because there will still be mortality, and there will still be sin. In fact, there will yet be one more sinful rebellion at the end of that glorious thousand years. God's people will still be waiting for the perfection of the eternal state.

The world has not yet seen anything like the Kingdom. Believers in the Church Age experience foreshadows of His earthly reign. Jesus is our King; He reigns in us; He is accomplishing His work in a broken world even now, giving us a foretaste of what is to come when He reigns. We have much to look forward to. That Golden Age depicted in Revelation 20 (and much of the rest of your Bible) is not the end; two chapters remain. Revelation 21 and 22 paint the picture of the Eternal State. "And He will wipe away every tear from their eyes; and there will no longer be any death; there will no longer be any mourning, or crying, or pain; the first things have passed away" (Revelation 21:4).

Even in the Millennial Kingdom, which will be as good as it has ever been—a perfect government and well-regulated citizenry under King Jesus' beautiful reign—even then, it is not yet done, and there is a better age coming. God is writing history on a trajectory headed towards a New Heaven and New Earth. Even the Millennial Kingdom is called "the first things," and it will pass according to Revelation 21:4. The Eternal State will come—our eternal rest—no more crying, no more night, no more sorrow, no more sickness, no more rebellion, no more sin.

God Waits

It is not just the created order that waits, but the Creator Himself who waits. Here are just a few examples:

God foretold that He would wait to rescue the Israelites from Egyptian slavery until the time was right. "Then in the fourth generation they will return here, for the iniquity of the Amorite is not yet complete" (Genesis 15:16). What was God saying? He was going to let the Amorites run the full course of their depravity and their rebellion so that he could judge them in greater fullness. He was going to let them have what they wanted. "Amorites, since you want to rebel against me, I'll give you what you want. I'll give you over to yourself." One of the worst things that could happen to you is that God would give you what you want, if it is not Him that you want. This is a judgment of God. And God waited until the sin of the Amorites was full until He brought the Israelites in to judge them.

We should be careful not to read the conquest narrative as if Israel's entrance into the land is a sinful, self-directed imperialistic genocide. The conquest of Palestine was under God's direction and God's control. This was part of His right dealings with sinful man. Every single one of us deserves to be a part of that conquest on the losing side. And God waited for the Amorites to express their sin to the fullest.

"Or do you think lightly of the riches of His kindness and tolerance and patience, not knowing that the kindness of God leads you to repentance?" (Romans 2:4). God is kind and patient toward rebels in order to bring the fullness of His kindness to them in His time. "And God, willing to demonstrate His wrath and to make His power known, endured with much patience vessels of wrath prepared for destruction" (Romans 9:22). All who are outside of Christ, who have not had their sins forgiven, are being prepared for destruction, and God is willing to make His power and His wrath known, to put on display His righteousness and the excellent beauties of His wrath. He endures with patience those vessels for destruction. There is a warning here for you who do not yet know God through His Son: repent, while there is still time. God waits. "Therefore the Lord longs to be gracious to you, And therefore He waits on high to have compassion on you. For the Lord is a God of justice; How blessed are all those who long for Him" (Isaiah 30:18). "The Lord is not slow about His promise, as some count slowness, but is patient toward you, not wishing for any to perish but for all to come to repentance" (2 Peter 3:9).

Jesus Waits

"I have come to cast fire upon the earth; and how I wish it were already kindled! But I have a baptism to undergo, and how distressed I am until it is accomplished!" (Luke 12:49–50). Jesus said this when He came the first time. This was a preview of His second coming. But He had a first-coming agenda to accomplish before He would judge the world. Jesus waited to bring righteous judgment. What did he wait for? He waited for the cross. Before He would judge the world for sin, He would Himself be judged for sin in order to redeem those who would believe. "But He, having offered one sacrifice for sins for all time, sat down at the right hand of God, waiting from that time onward until His enemies be made a footstool for His feet" (Hebrews 10:12–13). This has not yet been done. Jesus is still waiting.

We Wait

The Lord of hosts will prepare a lavish banquet for all peoples on this mountain; a banquet of aged wine, choice pieces with marrow, and refined, aged wine. And on this mountain He will swallow up the covering which is over all peoples, Even the veil which is stretched over all nations. He will swallow up death for all time, And the Lord God will wipe tears away from all faces, And He will remove the reproach of His people from all the earth; For the Lord has spoken. And it will be said in that day, 'Behold, this is our God for whom we have waited that He might save us. This is the Lord for whom we have waited; Let us rejoice and be glad in His salvation' (Isaiah 25:6–9).

This is one of my favorite passages in all of the Bible. As the people of God, what do we have to look forward to? A celebration begun (verse 6), the curse removed (verses 7-8), and God revealed (verse 9). The final culmination of our existence will be too good to be true, and we will no doubt feel the sentiment expressed by Richard Baxter: "Doubtless this will be our everlasting admiration, that so rich a crown should fit the head of so vile a sinner; that such high advancement, and such long unfruitfulness and unkindness, can be the state of the same person, and that such vile rebellions can conclude in such most precious joys!"[4] We wait for God, and our waiting for Him will not be in vain.

"This is our God for whom we have waited; Let us rejoice and be glad in His salvation!"

---

4 Richard Baxter, *The Saint's Everlasting Rest*, abridged by Benjamin Fawcett, 1856 edition (San Bernardino: ReadaClassic.com, 2013), 36. This is my favorite book about heaven.

WAITING ON GOD
WHEN LIFE IS HARD

This story appeared in *The New York Times* in August of 2012:

Some years ago, executives at a Houston airport faced a troubling customer-relations issue. Passengers were lodging an inordinate number of complaints about the long waits at baggage claim. In response, the executives increased the number of baggage handlers working that shift. The plan worked: the average wait fell to eight minutes, well within industry benchmarks. But the complaints persisted.

Puzzled, the airport executives undertook a more careful, on-site analysis. They found that it took passengers a minute to walk from their arrival gates to baggage claim and seven more minutes to get their bags. Roughly 88 percent of their time, in other words, was spent standing around waiting for their bags.

So the airport decided on a new approach: instead of reducing wait times, it moved the arrival gates away from the main terminal and routed bags to the outermost carousel.

Passengers now had to walk six times longer to get their bags. Complaints dropped to near zero.

Waiting is hard. Waiting is so hard for us that we would rather walk farther to retrieve our luggage, as long as we did not have to stand by the carousel for any amount of time to wait for our bags to come to us. Walking a mile is a better solution than twiddling our thumbs. Amusement parks have been known to overestimate wait times for rides, so that guests are pleasantly surprised when the wait is not as long as advertised.

Waiting is especially burdensome when life is difficult, when circumstances are hard and do not change, when there does not seem to be light at the end of the tunnel, when you are waiting for test results from the doctor, when you are looking for a new job, when you are trying to get into a college, when you are waiting for marriage or for children, or when you are waiting to find a good friend.

You may be sharing the gospel with a family member who is not responding. You may be trying to give counsel to a friend who is not listening, waiting for God by His Holy Spirit to change a life.

You wait when you are suffering under trial or even under discipline from God. You may be waiting under some sort of persecution. You may be grieving the death of a loved one, sorting out life without them, aching for eternity's reunion. Perhaps your home life is difficult. You may be a young man or a young woman who is having a hard time with your parents or your siblings. Maybe you find it challenging to love those under the same roof. Perhaps you find it challenging to give preference to others in love. In your unchanging circumstance, you must wait on God for His provision, His timing, His power, and His grace.

How Do I Wait on God?

What does it mean to wait on God? What does it look like? What does it feel like? What should I be doing? David, Israel's song-writer, gives the people of God a picture of what it means to wait on God in Psalm 37.

There is a duty, a discipline, and a delight in waiting. The duty is straight-forward: the command to "wait on God." That's a duty. We have an obligation before God to learn to wait on Him. There is also a discipline in it; waiting on God is hard, continual work. Waiting on God is not a one-time event that recalibrates your disposition for a life-time. No, you must shepherd your soul to a continual waiting on God when your circumstances do not change. But there is a delight in waiting, if the object of your waiting is God Himself. We're going to look at that sort of waiting here in Psalm 37. The first seven verses encapsulate all that is in the psalm. I would commend to you the entire psalm, but we will confine our study to the first seven verses.

Here is what David says:

Psalm 37:1–7

1   Do not fret because of evildoers,
    Be not envious toward wrongdoers.
2   For they will wither quickly like the grass
    And fade like the green herb.
3   Trust in Yahweh and do good;
    Dwell in the land and cultivate faithfulness.
4   Delight yourself in Yahweh;
    And He will give you the desires of your heart.
5   Commit your way to Yahweh,
    Trust also in Him, and He will do it.
6   He will bring forth your righteousness as the light
    And your judgment as the noonday.
7   Rest in Yahweh and wait patiently for Him;
    Do not fret because of him who prospers in his way,
    Because of the man who carries out wicked schemes.

Psalm 37 is a masterful poem, probably set to music. It is a unique poem—an acrostic, each stanza beginning with successive letters of the Hebrew alphabet. This song is like the ABCs of waiting on God when life is hard, and its arrangement would make its truths easier to remember. God must have known that His people would need the truths in this psalm. He certainly knew that I would need them.

Difficult circumstances lie behind this psalm. David is surrounded by people who do not love God but seem to have everything they want. They have not aligned themselves on the path that glorifies Yahweh, and yet they have material blessing and provision and apparent happiness and joy. Do you know this circumstance? Does it ever seem to you that the wicked have all the fun? That unwise and ungodly people seem to be blessed? Have you felt David's angst?

In verse 1, David says, "Do not fret because of evildoers, do not be envious of wrongdoers." If wrongdoers immediately got what they deserved, we would not envy them. We would not worry about them. David has to give us these commands: do not worry and do not envy. Why? Because wrongdoers aren't getting punished right away. You and I, who have perpetrated evil, know that we don't receive the full consequences of our actions right away. Solomon said, "Because the sentence against an evil deed is not executed quickly, therefore the hearts of the sons of men among them are given fully to do evil" (Ecclesiastes 8:11). David, like us, lives in a world in which many people do not run in the ways of God, yet they seem happy, lucky, healthy, and wealthy. He has focused his attention on the apparently favorable circumstances of godless people around him. In verse 16 David says, "Better is the little of the righteous than the abundance of many wicked." What is the dilemma in David's mind? Wicked people have abundance, and he has little. Notice verse 35: "I have seen a wicked, violent man spreading himself like a luxuriant tree in its native soil." This is a difficult circumstance. People who don't love God seem to have life going their way, and David's life is not going the way he thinks it should go.

Take the Long View of Circumstance

David opens the psalm with a string of commands. These commands proscribe duty, demand discipline, and promise delight. God tells us to do some things here, and thus failure to comply with these duties would be sin. The hard work of corralling our emotions requires a unique brand of discipline: relentless self-shepherding over time. But there is also delight in this disciplined duty—the delight of knowing God Himself.

The first instruction David gives for grappling with a difficult situation is to take the long view of your circumstance. This notion is found in the first two verses. When the godless seem to be experiencing all the blessing, "Do not fret," and "Be not envious." The word we translate "fret" carries the idea of being angry, agitated, or burning up with intense heat. Fretting and envying seem to be precisely the correct responses to the kind of injustice David portrays. If ever there was an opportunity for justifiable complaint, this is it. David instructs us, "Don't worry, and don't be jealous."

Only the long view can make sense of David's instructions, and the long view is exactly what David provides for us in verse 2: "They will wither quickly like grass and fade like the green herb." God knows we need more than a near-sighted perspective on this circumstance. You have a snap shot of what is happening right now. Watch the movie to see how the whole story goes. Skip to the end. Their good time is short. If you and I could measure the actual shortness of that good time compared with the infinite long-ness of eternity, there would not be words to describe the difference between them.

Destruction is coming. "They will wither quickly like the green grass and fade like the green herb" (verse 2). Without daily irrigation, the grass in my front yard would not stay green under the Arizona sun. My wife's basil plant survived two summer days without water. Destruction for the wicked approaches just as surely as green herb and the tender shoots wither under the heat of the desert sun.

Perhaps you are like the grass in Psalm 37. If your current existence is hunky dory, if your life right now seems to be going well, and you are not on Yahweh's path—you need to know that destruction is coming, and your good time is short. This is a promise from the God who created you and who has the end in sight.

For those of us who know God, this command is simple. Don't envy those who are marked out for destruction. Why would you envy the grass that springs up in a day and withers in the next? Such envy is suicidal: "Wow! Look how green that grass is! How much fun would it be to be a blade of grass with no water in the Arizona sun!" Don't envy the life that is in the cross-hairs of God's righteous judgment. Take the long view.

Do you have this perspective when you walk the halls at school? Do you have this view among your colleagues at work, when everyone is talking about the stuff they have and the things that they do and all their fun times without God? Do you envy their lives? Do you worry that you are not getting your reward?

How does your heart handle delayed gratification? The Christian lives a life of delayed gratification. You and I have been promised grand things we have not yet received and will not receive in this life. We have down-payments, hints, and foretastes, but we do not yet have fulfillment. This temporal existence is not our home. The Christian life, fundamentally, is a pilgrimage of delayed gratification. You were saved to wait, and your heart must be shepherded to handle delayed gratification.

I have an exceptionally difficult time waiting for things that God

Himself says are good. For instance, God says that marriage is good, a picture of the Gospel for the world to see, and that a single Christian ought to prepare herself or himself to be a godly spouse. Countless godly people have gone before into the joys and benefits and sanctification available in marriage. Why then are some godly people not married? Why must some wait a long time to get married? God's Word tells us that children are a blessing from Him, that full quivers are strategic. Cute little bundles of depravity become captive audience for years of evangelism and discipleship, and they provide opportunities for growth in selfless sacrifice and Christ-likeness. If having children is good, then why must some wait? Some couples try for years to have just one child, while others seem to be quite fertile without trying. Many mothers, ignorantly or with full knowledge, participate in our nation's holocaust, sacrificing their own children on the altars of convenience, self-advancement, or sin. Meanwhile, godly parents watch on and wonder, "Why won't God give us the baby we long for?" God says that a good friend is a valuable commodity. Why is He making me wait so long to find one? If the salvation of my children, a loved one, a neighbor, or a friend would be a good thing, why must I wait? Waiting on God for "good" things is especially difficult. And yet the instruction remains: trust God and wait.

Trust God and His Plan

David, in verse 3, gives God's people a second instruction for waiting on God in difficult situations, "Trust in Yahweh and do good; Dwell in the land and cultivate faithfulness." This is a two-pronged command: we are to put our confidence in a person and a plan. The person is Yahweh ("LORD" in all-capital letters in our English Bible stands for the Hebrew YHWH, or Yahweh). "God" is a title for the supreme deity, much like "President" is a title, but Yahweh is His personal name, most likely derived from the Hebrew verb "to be." God revealed Himself by this name to Moses in Exodus 3:14: "God said to Moses, 'I AM WHO I AM'; and He said, 'Thus you shall say to the sons of Israel, "I AM has sent me to you."'" God's name proclaims His own self-existence; He is the One who created everything from nothing. As the only uncreated, independent being, He just is. Everything else that exists is totally dependent upon Him. The One who is life in Himself gives life to all whom He chooses. God said to Israel, in effect, "I want you to know Me by name, because I am Yahweh, and I keep my promises." Yahweh is the self-existent, covenant-keeping God of Israel who enters into personal relationship with His people. This is the meaning of His name Yahweh. He is the One with whom we have to do, and He is to be the object of our trust.

It is no linguistic accident that when the Old Testament was translated into Greek (the language that was spoken at the time of Jesus), the name "Yahweh" was translated into the Greek word for "Lord." In the New Testament, the designation most often given to Jesus is the word "Lord," a reflection of the Hebrew name "Yahweh." This indicates something startling about God's intent in sending His Son Jesus to earth. Here is the image of God in man. Here is the full representation of the Father in a human being who is 100% God and 100% man, and He came to bring us unmediated relationship to the God of the universe. God took on flesh precisely so that we could know Him. To know Jesus is to know Yahweh. You cannot know God except through the Son, Yahweh in the flesh.

Yahweh is the person in whom we trust. And we are also to trust His plan. Notice what David says in verse 3: "Trust in Yahweh and do good." Do good. Obedience to God is a reflection of your trust in Him. When we obey God's commands, we are in effect saying, "God, that's a good idea. You are good, and You do good. I trust You, and so I will follow Your directions."

David spells out God's plan in verse 3: "Dwell in the land and cultivate faithfulness." That is an interesting couple of commands. God's people were at this time living in Israel under the kingly rule of David himself. They already live in the land, and David says, "live there." You might think me strange if I directed a Phoenix resident to live in Phoenix. What does David mean?

This is a song for Israel, penned by David in the land. His command is this: enjoy God's plan for you. At this time, they are living in the land that God had promised under the king that God had provided, and David says to them, "trust in that plan." Resist the temptation to envy greener grass elsewhere. God has made bountiful provision for you. Dwell in that provision. Live here. Abide in the land. Enjoy God's provision.

The second part of that command is "cultivate faithfulness.» The phrase literally reads, "pasture faithfulness." A farmer's field is turned into a verb, and the resulting phrase means one of two things. First, to "pasture faithfulness" could mean to cultivate fidelity to God in your life. Like a farmer diligently cultivates his crops, you are to diligently cultivate faithfulness in your own life towards God. Or secondly, to "pasture faithfulness" could mean that you are to graze on God's loyalty to you, like a cow in the field, eating the food that is there. God's covenant loyalty is available everywhere you turn, so you go graze on that. Both ideas are good, but only one of them is right. I will leave you with the interpretive decision.

The aim of this text is to encourage God's people to trust God's plan. Waiting on God is trust multiplied by time. Do you possess that capacity? Do you have the discipline in your life to rest in the situation in which God has placed you? Is it a discipline that you have

Cultivate faithfulness

Gods Plan for me is perfect have hope in that

cultivated? Do you know Yahweh well enough to trust Him? You and I are not the nation of Israel; we do not live in the land and are not ruled by King David. But there is a principle here for us. God is our God, and He has a plan for our good and for His glory. Dwell where God has placed you, content with the good He has provided for you.

Delight in Yahweh

David gives God's people another instruction for waiting on God when life is hard: "Delight in Yahweh; And He will give you the desires of your heart" (Psalm 37:4). A command and a promise take aim at our emotions. Have you ever heard it said, "I can't change how I feel"? Guess what ... here in your Bible is a command to do just that. This is a command from God to change how you feel. Direct your affections, and God will give you the desires of your heart. As a seventeen-year-old, I thought this verse promised me a Lamborghini Countach. Blank check! If I get this delight-in-God thing right, I can get whatever I want! It's a promise! This *is* a promise, but it is not a promise from God to fulfill my idolatrous fancies. This promise is so much better!

If the Lamborghini is the goal, then God is penultimate at best. He is a genie in a bottle waiting for me to rub the lamp just right so that he can fulfill my wishes. Frankly, this is the view most people have of God. In pursuit of rusting trinkets and cracker-jack treasures, people will religiously placate their self-styled version of God. However, if God Himself is the treasure to be pursued, then the person who delights himself in Yahweh will get exactly what his heart desires! The great secret of the universe is this: only Yahweh can come through on the promise to delight the heart! And He delights to come through on that promise! Everything else that brings delight suffers creation's disease, slavery to corruption. Everything "under the sun" is programmed to decay, rust, fall apart, fail, and die (see Romans 8:20-21 and Ecclesiastes 7:13). You cannot un-curse what God has cursed. Any created thing that promises lasting happiness is a liar and the truth is not in it. Created things do not have that kind of power. While all good things come from God, the things themselves do not have the power to satisfy. True and lasting satisfaction is God's alone to give (Ecclesiastes 5:19). God deserves and demands the ultimate place in our affections. Anything less is idolatry.

The unbelievably good command and promise from God is simple: delight yourself in Yahweh, and you will find the desires of your heart fulfilled. I am a little older than seventeen now, and I know that God is better than a Lamborghini. In fact, I know that God invented metal, rubber, and roads and the people that designed engines. Knowing and being loved by the Inventor of "fun" is infinitely superior to possessing any single "good" thing. Should the kid desire the toy or the toy maker? This notion is a fundamental difference between biblical Christianity and everything else out there. We desire, delight in, pursue, and treasure a Person, and that Person is committed to our delight. Isn't that fascinating? The God that we pursue is committed to our enjoyment in Him. So make God the delight of your heart, and you will have your heart's desire.

Why does God have us wait on Him? Is it so that we can get married? Is it so that we can have children? Is it so that we can get into college? Is it so that we can find a friend? Is it so that my little brother will stop pestering me? Is it so that my financial troubles will disappear? Or is it so that we can have Him? David knew that knowing God is the greatest good. If you cultivate love for God in your heart, you will never be disappointed. No circumstance, no trial, no adversity, no surprise, no situation can take Yahweh away from you when your desire is set on Him. Nothing else comes with that guarantee.

Everything else can be lost! Ask Job. If your treasure is something less than God, you are vulnerable. Do you understand? Do you believe it in your gut? If something other than God is your treasure, you will sway like a kelp stalk in the shifting tides of happenstance. But if God is the Rock on which you have stayed your heart, you will never be moved.

The Christian's rewards are not all in heaven. Even in this life God gives His children measures of delight and fun and enjoyment. Every temporal enjoyment is supposed to be a hint of what awaits us in His glorious presence. Delighting in Yahweh does not demand that we eschew fun; delighting in Yahweh demands that we worship Him in our earthly enjoyments, seeking first the One who is the Source of true joy. Enjoy a great meal! Rejoice in good times with friends. But it must all happen under the banner of worship. If you cannot worship Jesus and have fun, you are doing the wrong thing or pursuing it in the wrong way. God has designed "under the sun" delights (to borrow Solomon's label for earthly goods) to be an appetizer to whet our appetites for the feast of delights to come.

How do you manage unpleasant circumstances that refuse to change? Delight yourself in Yahweh, and He will give you the desires of your heart.

Turn Your Life Over To God

"Commit your way to Yahweh, Trust also in Him, and He will do it. He will bring forth your righteousness as the light And your judgment as the noonday" (Psalm 37:5–6). David's fourth instruction for waiting on God when life is hard is about surrender. You must give up. You must turn the control of your life over to Him. "Commit your way to Yahweh." If God is not driving, you are in trouble; this will not end well. Let God have it. Trust Him. The Hebrew here says, "trust Him, He will do." Quite simply, God will accomplish all that is right and good, whatever is most in keeping with His glory, whatever is best. You and I are terrible assessors of what is best, and we not good at making the best a reality. God is really good at both.

Have you ever feared God's control? Have you longed for some guarantee up front that God will steer this right if you hand over the controls? Think about this for a moment. What might such fear be revealing about your heart? Is it possible that you have a white-knuckled grip on some idolatrous affection? Surrendering to God would mean bringing your life under the direction of His Word. That might cost you something you are unwilling to lose. Might the fear of surrender actually be revealing wayward affections? If you are afraid to relinquish control over the direction, priorities, and commitments of your life, you are likely entertaining idolatry.

I recommend a cost-benefit analysis. What does an idol demand from you, and what does that idol provide in return? The reality is that love of anything more than God will actually destroy you, no matter what it may promise. If your career path directs your decisions, shapes your priorities, and demands your sacrifices, you will one day wake to discover that your "god" is not able to deliver on the satisfaction, fulfillment, and joy that it promised. God alone has the power to supply true joy, satisfaction, and fulfillment; these things will forever elude those who surrender to lesser gods.

Hear God's Word. Listen to His promise. "Commit your way to the Yahweh; Trust also in Him, and He will do it. He will bring forth your righteousness as the light And your judgment as the noonday." David tells us that there is vindication in the end. Your life right now may be filled with shadows; life's vibrancy may have dimmed to barely distinguishable gray hues in the twilight of a long trial. This certainly does not feel like noonday sun. God promises that light is coming. He just does not tell us when. My heart is often troubled by this uncertainty, but my troubled heart must hear from God, "Trust Me. Wait."

Wait on God

"Rest in Yahweh and wait patiently for Him" (Psalm 37:7). David's circumstances are vexing. He is troubled by the inequity that he sees around him. Godless people experience blessing, while the godly suffer. What is to be done? What is David's recommendation for managing life when circumstances are difficult? One might expect for the king to take matters into his own hands. Instead, he recommends, "rest" and "wait," silently and patiently. This command is a duty, a discipline, and a delight. David describes an attitude in waiting on God. Patient waiting on God is not idleness. David has in view an active captivation of his thoughts. Resting and waiting on God means telling your heart what to feel, telling your soul what to do, and telling your brain how to think.

David's initial command is "rest." To rest means to silence your complaining heart, to cease floundering. Rest in Yahweh. Then he instructs us to "wait patiently." Restless impatience reveals idolatry in the heart. Do you want to find out what you love and trust more than God? Observe your patience. Notice what draws out impatience in you. Impatience demonstrates what you love and in whom you trust. Our sovereign God has ordained every path and simultaneously loves His children with infinite and unflinching love. He knows all things, and He controls all things for His glory and our good. We can wait. Patience and impatience proclaim theology. Waiting on God is a declaration that He is good, sovereign, and omniscient. My impatience proclaims, perhaps more loudly than my credal statements to the contrary, that God is not good, that He is not truly in control, that He doesn't really know everything, or that He does not have my best interests at heart.

When we wait well in difficult circumstances, God supplies the grace of rest in Him, and we find that we get everything that we really need. Remarkably, when circumstances favorably change, we discover that the favorable circumstance that we wanted is not nearly as good as the person of God. And that is the point. Paul Tripp said this about waiting on God:

> Waiting on God isn't about the suspension of meaning and purpose. It's part of the meaning and purpose that God has brought into my life. Waiting on God isn't to be viewed as an obstruction in the way of the plan. Waiting is an essential part of the plan. For the child of God, waiting isn't simply about what I'll receive at the end of my wait. No, waiting is much more purposeful, efficient, and practical than that. Waiting is fundamentally about what I'll become as I wait. God is using the wait to do in me and through me exactly what He's promised. Through the wait He's changing me. By means of the wait He's altering the fabric of my thoughts and desires. Through the wait He's causing me to see and experience new things about Him and His kingdom. And all of this sharpens me, enabling me to be a more useful tool in His redemptive hands.[5]

Where does biblical waiting come from? Can you muster it up yourself? Is this ability inside you somewhere, just waiting to be drawn up from the stores of your own inherent abilities? Can you just determine to wait? Asking me to produce biblical waiting on God is like requesting a drink from a septic tank. I can't produce it. You can't

---

5 Paul David Tripp, *A Shelter in The Storm: Meditations on God and Trouble* (Wheaton: Crossway Books, 2009), 143.

make it. Biblical waiting only comes from new birth, from the regenerating power of the Holy Spirit and His resulting love, joy, peace, and patience.... It is what the Holy Spirit produces in the heart of one who belongs to God. He does it by taking someone who is dead in transgressions and sins and making them alive. Supernatural power is required for waiting on God.

Is your life is loaded with complaining impatience? Do you believe your life is out of control? Are you convinced that everything wrong around you is someone else's fault? Are you unable to make heads or tails of your circumstance? Do you find yourself perpetually asking "When is this ever going to end? When do I get to be in charge?" If so, you may have a fundamental question to ask yourself, "Am I born from above? Have I experienced new birth?" The Christian life is all about waiting on God. God produces the supply that the believer needs by His Holy Spirit in the heart. Believers must cultivate it and discipline themselves to pursue it. But fundamentally, it comes from God, and if you don't have it, it is a sign that you do not know Him.

If you don't know Jesus, you will forever be the victim of your circumstances. Your station in life, the people around you, and the things that happen to you will be masters over you, and you will be enslaved. The new creature in Jesus is free, free to trust the sovereign God of the universe who orders everything for the good of those who love Him.

God is the one who gives perseverance (Romans 15:5); He is called "the God of hope" (Romans 15:13); and He is the one who gives us hope by His grace (2 Thessalonians 2:16). In Colossians 1:11, Paul prays that believers "would be strengthened with all power, according to His glorious might, for the attaining of all steadfastness and patience." Waiting is all over the Bible, and God is the source and the supplier of all biblical waiting. So go to God; pray, depend, and wait on Him.

WAIT

by Russell Kelfer

Desperately, helplessly, longingly, I cried;
Quietly, patiently, lovingly, God replied.
I pled and I wept for a clue to my fate...
And the Master so gently said, "Wait."
Wait? You say wait? my indignant reply.
Lord, I need answers, I need to know why!
Is Your hand shortened? Or have You not heard?
By faith I have asked, and I'm claiming Your Word.
My future and all to which I relate
Hangs in the balance, and You tell me to wait?
I'm needing a 'yes,' a go-ahead sign.
Or even a 'no,' to which I'll resign.
You promised, dear Lord, that if we believe,
We need but to ask, and we shall receive.
Lord, I've been asking, and this is my cry:
I'm weary of asking! I need a reply.
Then quietly, softly, I learned of my fate,
As my Master replied again, "Wait."
So I slumped in my chair, defeated and taut,
And grumbled to God, So I'm waiting... for what?
He seemed then to kneel, and His eyes met with mine...
And He tenderly said, I could give you a sign.
I could shake the heavens and darken the sun.
I could raise the dead and cause mountains to run.
I could give all you seek and pleased you would be.
You'd have what you want, but you wouldn't know Me.

You'd not know the depth of My love for each saint.
You'd not know the power that I give to the faint.
You'd not learn to see through clouds of despair;
You'd not learn to trust just by knowing I'm there.
You'd not know the joy of resting in Me
When darkness and silence are all you can see.
You'd never experience the fullness of love
When the peace of My spirit descends like a dove.
You would know that I give, and I save, for a start,
But you'd not know the depth of the beat of My heart,
The glow of My comfort late into the night,
The faith that I give when you walk without sight,
The depth that's beyond getting just what you ask
From an infinite God who makes what you have last.
You'd never know should your pain quickly flee,
What it means that My grace is sufficient for thee.
Yes, your dearest dreams overnight would come true,
But, oh, the loss, if you missed what I'm doing in you.
So be silent, my child, and in time you will see
That the greatest of gifts is to truly know Me.
And though oft My answers seem terribly late,
My most precious answer of all is still… "Wait."[6]

---

6 Russell Kelfer was a San Antonio businessman and church lay leader who left the land of the dying in 2000.

WHAT DO I DO
WHILE I WAIT?

Think about the last time you were at the Motor Vehicle Division. Or the last time you were in a waiting room in a doctor's office. What did you do while you waited? Did you play a game on your smartphone? Did you report to your social media followers? Maybe you read a magazine. Maybe you found people to talk to. There are times when we are forced to wait, when we feel like the task at hand is to kill time. Do you ever feel like you're killing time or that you are waiting for something to happen?

I lived my elementary school years in Alaska. My parents often purchased Christmas presents from catalogs. Toys purchased from catalogs had to be shipped. You may have noticed the fine print on mail-order delivery for certain products: "shipping available to 48 states." Well, the state I lived in was not one of those 48, and Christmas packages tended to arrive in mid-January. Perhaps you can imagine the angst of a nine-year-old waiting for a remote-control truck to arrive, sent by mail to the end of the earth. Christmas was late several years in a row.

Every remaining day of Christmas vacation found that nine-year-old boy staring out the window waiting for the mailman to show up at the mailbox. Is he here yet? Is he here yet? Finally, the mailman! Is there a little, yellow note that's going to tell me I can go to the post office and pick up a package? No, not yet. Eventually, school started up again. I didn't want to go to school! I wanted to wait for the mailman! My parents helped me discover something rather remarkable: one can wait for the mailman AND go to school.

Waiting on God is not some sort of sanctified slumber or Christian coma. The Christian life is defined by waiting. Following Jesus is a life of deferred gratification. That is, we don't receive, in this life, everything we're promised. And so we wait on God. Getting God is the primary purpose of waiting. When we elevate a change in circumstances above a clinging to God Himself, we have missed the point of biblical waiting. Yet, waiting is not about inactivity. While we wait on God, while we wait for Jesus' return, what are we supposed to do?

In Luke 12, with three stories, Jesus teaches us how to wait for His return. There is a story about slaves who await a master's return from a wedding feast at night, a story about a homeowner not expecting to be robbed, and a story about a manager who waits for the boss.

Slaves Awaiting Their Master's Return at Night

Be dressed in readiness, and keep your lamps lit. Be like men who are waiting for their master when he returns from the wedding feast, so that they may immediately open the door to him when he comes and knocks. Blessed are those slaves whom the master will find on the alert when he comes; truly I say to you, that he will gird himself to serve, and have them recline at the table, and will come up and wait on them. Whether he comes in the second watch, or even in the third, and finds them so, blessed are those slaves (Luke 12:35–38).

How are we to await the return of Jesus? Like slaves awaiting their master's return at night, dressed in readiness with lamps lit. To be dressed in readiness is literally "to have a belted waist." In the ancient near east, long flowing garments were commonly worn for their comfort, but they were not very conducive for movement. You tied up your loose garments with a belt, making yourself ready for activity. Implicit in this directive is anticipation on the part of the servants. Something is going to happen, my services are going to be needed, my master may come at any point and knock on the door, and I need to be belted at the waist. I need to be dressed in readiness. I need to have my affairs, my garments, in order so that I am ready for my master when he comes.

Additionally, Jesus tells His disciples, "keep your lamps lit." The master may return in the first, second, or third watch of the night. This is normally the time for sleep, but these servants are to be dressed with their lamps lit. The servants are to be "on the alert" (verse 37). One doesn't know when the master will come back. How long is this wedding feast to go on? How long will he entertain his guests? How long will the conversations go? But when he knocks, be ready. Wait in readiness.

The faithful servant would eagerly anticipate the master's return. The faithful servant should rejoice at seeing his master, ready to open the door. The servant does not serve himself, but the master. Jesus says to His followers, "be like those slaves." The master is away, He will be returning, and we don't know when. We must be servants who wait in readiness.

A Homeowner [Not] Expecting a Burglar

How are we to await Jesus' return? Jesus gave His disciples a second story in Luke 12, of a homeowner expecting, or perhaps not expecting, a burglar. "But be sure of this, that if the head of the house had known at what hour the thief was coming, he would not have allowed his house to be broken into. You too, be ready; for the Son of Man is coming at an hour that you do not expect" (Luke 12:39–40).

What would do if you arrived at your home one afternoon to find the following note attached to your front door?

> Dear Homeowner:
> I am planning to burgle this residence tonight at 11:45 PM.
>
> —Clep.

Would you call the police? Would you bar the doors and check the windows? You might arm yourself or hide your most precious possessions. Perhaps you would spend time meditating on the transient nature of stuff—"if the thief doesn't break in and steal it, the moths or the rust will be sure to get it. It's just stuff." Maybe you would place your valuables by the front door, strategically stuffed with Gospel tracts and paperback New Testaments. Whatever you did, you probably wouldn't sleep. This would certainly not be a routine evening. You would be at a heightened level of readiness, preparing the best way you knew. Jesus tells His disciples that they do not know when He will return anymore than a homeowner knows when a burglar is going to burgle. Be on the alert.

A Manager Waiting for the Boss

Peter said, 'Lord, are You addressing this parable to us, or to everyone else as well?' And the Lord said, 'Who then is the faithful and sensible steward, whom his master will put in charge of his servants, to give them their rations at the proper time? Blessed is that slave whom his master finds so doing when he comes. Truly I say to you that he will put him in charge of all his possessions. But if that slave says in his heart, "My master will be a long time in coming," and begins to beat the slaves, both men and women, and to eat and drink and get drunk; the master of that slave will come on a day when he does not expect him and at an hour he does not know, and will cut him in pieces, and assign him a place with the unbelievers. And that slave who knew his master's will and did not get ready or act in accord with his will, will receive many lashes, but the one who did not know it, and committed deeds worthy of a flogging, will receive but few. From everyone who has been given much, much will be required; and to whom they entrusted much, of him they will ask all the more' (Luke 12:41–48).

Before Jesus tells the third story, Peter interrupts the lesson with a question, "Lord, are you addressing this parable to us, or to everyone else as well?" Jesus' answer to Peter's question is, "Who is the faithful and sensible steward?" This doesn't really sound like an answer to the question. In fact, there seems to be a disconnect between most of Jesus' answers and the questions that prompted them. Jesus routinely answered the question that people should have been asking, rather than the question that actually escaped their lips. Peter asks, "Are you talking to them or us?" And Jesus says, "Who is the faithful steward?" You and I could ask, "Jesus, were you talking to Peter? Or to people in the first century?" And Jesus answers, "Who is the faithful steward?" Jesus broadens the application of the lesson. The faithful steward is going to be the one who hears and heeds this story. This story is for us, if we have ears to hear it.

Jesus' third story is the tale of a manager who waits for the boss. The boss is away; the manager is managing his boss's business, and he awaits the boss's return. The job of the manager ("steward") is to care for the affairs of this household—the slaves, the servants, and all of the activities. A faithful steward (verse 42) gives the workers their rations at the proper time. He makes certain that the needs of the household are met appropriately. That faithful and sensible steward (verse 43) is blessed. And notice what Jesus says in verse 43, "blessed is that slave who the master finds so doing." That slave is waiting for the master's return, but his waiting is not in idleness. He waits in faithful doing. On display here is a disposition of waiting that manifests itself in urgent obedience. He is a faithful and sensible steward, doing what he is supposed to be doing at the time he is supposed to be doing it. And he will be blessed for his fidelity to his master's will. Jesus promises a reward for such servants, "Truly I say to you that he will put him in charge of all his possessions" (verse 44).

A contrast emerges in verse 45. What if the household steward was not faithful or sensible? What if the manager was delinquent instead? What if he neglected his master's will and established his own agenda? "My master has not come yet, and it's been a long time already, and no one knows the day or the hour of his return, so we may as well eat, drink, and be merry. I can live however I want. Be lazy. Carouse. Act like a tyrant. I should be the boss for a while." The problem with the wicked slave's short-sighted plan is that the master is coming back. In verse 46, Jesus says that the master of that slave will come on a day when he does not expect him, at an hour when he does not know, will cut him in pieces and assign him a place with the unbelievers. Wow, this story just took a nasty turn! The master in the story has seriously overreacted. For a little drunken disorderliness, the boss went slasher-movie on his manager!

Do you see what happened in verse 46? Jesus has transitioned from story to reality, almost seamlessly. In verse 45, we think we are still listening to a story; Jesus is talking about a slave and a master. In verse 46, He is still talking about the master of that slave, but this little word at the end of verse 46, "unbelievers," lets us know that Jesus is talking about something much more significant than an earthly employer-employee relationship. He is talking about eternal realities here. He has elevated the story above master-slave to Creator-creature. Jesus has in His sights real people answering for their lives to Almighty God.

Everyone of us has been endowed by God with time, gifts, responsibilities, and opportunities; and every one of us has squandered them. Each of us needs a rescue, a salvation. The blood of God the Son Himself is required to pay for all of our rebellious squandering, to pay for all the wasted time, to pay for every evil deed and every evil thought.

Why does the master assign the wicked slave a place with the "unbelievers"? "Unbeliever" is an interesting name to call someone who works for you. It is not as if this slave did not think this master existed. It is not as if he did not live and work within his household. But he gets cast out as an unbeliever because of what his actions reveal about his heart. The wicked slave treasured revelry and carousing and laziness and self-promotion above serving his master. Those are manifestations of unbelief.

In verse 47, Jesus describes the slave who knew his master's will and did not get ready or act in accord with his will. That slave will receive many lashes, and the one who did not know his master's will, committing deeds worthy of a flogging, will receive few. What is Jesus saying here? Again, He is outside the story; Jesus is describing eternal realities and real people. There are degrees of punishment in hell. Not everybody gets the same treatment in eternal destruction. Make no mistake; verses 47 and 48 are about hell—the irreversible, eternal outpouring of God's infinite wrath on everyone who is not in Christ. But it is not the same for everybody. Those who have heard truth, who have been exposed to truth, who have been given more responsibilities and more opportunities, will receive greater punishment. Jesus closes with a sober warning: "to whom they entrusted much, of him they will ask all the more."

Twiddling Our Thumbs?

What does this eternal perspective say about the kind of waiting that we must do? Waiting for Jesus is not comatose. In fact, a faithful Christian life is a flurry of activity. Consider the Apostle Paul, who taught us much about what it means to persevere, to endure, to hope, to trust, to wait, to eagerly anticipate Jesus' return. Paul ran hard. He said, "I endure all things for the sake of those who are chosen, so that they may obtain the salvation which is in Christ Jesus and with it eternal life" (2 Timothy 2:10). He knew what it was to wait, and his waiting was marked by urgent obedience, as if people's eternal destinies depended on his urgent proclamation of the gospel.

Waiting is not inactivity. Waiting is an attitude, a posture. You can be very busy and have a waiting disposition. It is an attitude of trust, anticipation, hope, longing, obedience, faith, endurance, and confidence. We rest in God, and we trust His plan. Such trust results in urgent obedience, because we want to be found pleasing to our Master when He returns.

If you thought that waiting on God required some sort of thumb-twiddling contest to pass the time, I want to offer you a list. This is a list of activities given to us by God in His Word, things to do while we wait. Most of them come from the New Testament. As Jesus departed, He gave His disciples a commission: to "make disciples of all the nations, baptizing..., teaching them to observe all that I commanded you" (Matthew 28:19-20). Until I return, make more followers. Baptize them and teach them to do what I told you. The New Testament records the instructions believers are to follow as we wait for our Lord's return. For the sake of not repeating the entire New Testament in this chapter, I have summarized a list of commands that come from passages infused with waiting vocabulary and waiting themes.

What should I do while I wait? Below is a lengthy list of commands from waiting-on-God contexts. You may peruse this list any way you like: skim the list, carefully read each listed command, or study each of the passages in detail. Whatever you choose, I think you will be overwhelmed at God's expectation of what we should be doing while we wait on Him.

- Serve God (1 Thessalonians 1:9-10; Romans 12:6-21)
- Labor and strive for godliness (1 Timothy 4:7-10)
- Do good (Psalm 37:3)
- Cultivate faithfulness (Psalm 37:3)
- Delight yourself in Yahweh (Psalm 37:4)
- Commit your way to Yahweh (Psalm 37:5)
- Keep His way (Psalm 37:34)
- Give thanks (Psalm 52:9; Colossians 1:9-11)
- Follow the way of God's judgments (Isaiah 26:8-9)
- Long for God (Isaiah 26:8-9)
- Seek God (Isaiah 26:8-9; Lamentations 3:25)
- Remember God (Isaiah 26:8-9)
- Return to God (Hosea 12:6)
- Observe kindness and justice (Hosea 12:6)
- Preach [a command for pastors] (2 Timothy 4:2)
- Run the race set out for you by God (Hebrews 12:1)
- Lay aside encumbrances and sin (Hebrews 12:1)
- Fix your eyes on Jesus (Hebrews 12:1)

- Prepare your minds for action (1 Peter 1:13)
- Keep sober in spirit (1 Peter 1:13)
- Fix your hope on coming grace (1 Peter 1:13)
- Strengthen your heart (James 5:8)
- Hope in God's Word (Psalm 130:5)
- Pray [a godly widow's relentless prayer demonstrates hopeful waiting on God] (1 Timothy 5:5)
- Be strong. Let your heart take courage (Psalm 27:14)
- Build yourselves up in the faith (Jude 20-21)
- Pray in the Holy Spirit (Jude 20-21)
- Keep yourself in the love of God (Jude 20-21)
- Be filled with the knowledge of God's will (Colossians 1:9-11)
- Be filled with spiritual understanding and wisdom (Colossians 1:9-11)
- Walk in a manner worthy of the Lord (Colossians 1:9-11)
- Please God in everything (Colossians 1:9-11)
- Bear fruit in every good work (Colossians 1:9-11)
- Grow in your knowledge of God (Colossians 1:9-11)
- Be strengthened with all power (Colossians 1:9-11)
- Work hard like a farmer (1 Corinthians 9:10)
- Speak boldly (2 Corinthians 3:12)
- Love other Christians (Colossians 1:4-5)
- Deny ungodliness and worldly desires (Titus 2:12)
- Live sensibly, righteously, and godly (Titus 2:12)
- Hold fast your confession of hope (Hebrews 10:23)
- Stimulate one another to love and good deeds (Hebrews 10:24)
- Assemble together (Hebrews 10:25)
- Encourage one another (Hebrews 10:25)
- Do what is right (1 Peter 4:19)

- Use your gifts in the church (Romans 12:6-21)
- Love genuinely (Romans 12:6-21)
- Abhor evil (Romans 12:6-21)
- Cling to what is good (Romans 12:6-21)
- Be devoted to one another in brotherly love (Romans 12:6-21)
- Give preference to one another in honor (Romans 12:6-21)
- Be fervent in spirit (Romans 12:6-21)
- Rejoice! (Romans 12:6-21)
- Persevere in tribulation (Romans 12:6-21)
- Be devoted to prayer (Romans 12:6-21)
- Give to the needs of Christians (Romans 12:6-21)
- Practice hospitality (Romans 12:6-21)
- Bless persecutors (Romans 12:6-21)
- Rejoice with those who rejoice (Romans 12:6-21)
- Weep with those who weep (Romans 12:6-21)
- Be like-minded with one another (Romans 12:6-21)
- Associate with the lowly (Romans 12:6-21)
- Respect what is right in the sight of all men (Romans 12:6-21)
- As far as possible with you, be at peace with all men (Romans 12:6-21)
- Be kind to your enemies (Romans 12:6-21)
- Overcome evil with good (Romans 12:6-21)

God also gives some instructions about what *not* to do while we wait:
- Fret (Psalm 37:7)
- Complain against one another (James 5:9)
- Give yourself to wanton pleasure (1 Timothy 5:6)
- Lose heart (2 Corinthians 4:16-18)
- Complain against God (Lamentations 3:26, 39)

- Be lazy (Romans 12:11-12)
- Curse those who persecute you (Romans 12:12-14)
- Be arrogant (Romans 12:16)
- Be wise in your own estimation (Romans 12:16)
- Pay back evil for evil (Romans 12:17)
- Take your own revenge (Romans 12:19)
- Be overcome by evil (Romans 12:21)
- Sin (Do you need a reference?)

The commands and prohibitions above come from contexts in which "waiting," "hoping," "exercising patience," and "enduring" are specifically mentioned. And since waiting on God is a fundamental disposition of the Christian life, every command for believers in the New Testament could be added to this list.

How are you waiting? What is your attitude when you are forced to wait for your circumstances to change? How have you arranged your earthly existence to come into conformity with the way Jesus says He wants His disciples to wait? Are your garments belted in readiness? Have you arranged your affairs so that you can answer the door when He knocks, so that you are ready when the Master comes? Or will Jesus' unexpected return find you unprepared, disobedient, and not waiting for Him?

WAITING ON GOD
IN MY FIGHT WITH SIN

The impulse buy is one of the tragic side effects of disposable income. How many times have you disposed of your income impulsively, only to feel the pain of buyer's remorse before you even made it out of the parking lot? Think of all the time and money spent on junk hurriedly acquired before your brain, your budget, or your significant other could get a protest in edgewise.

The worst kind of impulse buy involves food. You know the drill: you see something that looks really good, your midsection growls, the stomach-to-eye size ratio is way out of whack, and you find yourself ordering a double portion of whatever it is you should have skipped altogether. When it's all done, money is lost, calories are gained, and the anticipation of delight has turned to bloated agony.

Sin is the ultimate impulse buy. Sin is the king of false advertising. Sin makes promises it cannot possibly keep, telling us that enjoyment is available if only we would set aside what we know and buy now. NOW. And sin never delivers. Instead of lasting happiness, only emptiness follows.

Consider several examples. Think about sinful anger. In the moment, sinful anger seems justifiable, right, appropriate, and effective. If I just get angry right now, raise my voice, and elevate the intensity, my point will be made. Things will be accomplished. But my sinful anger invariably exacerbates bad situations. Consider the sin of impatience. Impatience seems like a fitting response to a world moving much too slowly, but it never accomplishes what it promises. Likewise, sexual immorality, for all of its promises, only leaves emptiness, pain, and regret.

Temptations to sin are everywhere in the world around us and inside us. For the non-Christian, who is by definition a slave of sin and categorically enveloped in sin, this reality does not usually create tension[7]. In the way that a fish does not "feel wet," a sinner does not necessarily "feel sin." There is no battlefield of intentions for the one for whom "every intention of the thoughts of the heart is only evil continually" (Genesis 6:5). Outside of Christ, no one does good (Romans 3:10-18). In fact, the best that a sinful man outside of Christ has to offer is trash before God (Isaiah 64:6; Philippians 3:8).

The Christian has come to Christ to flee from sin, to have conscience cleansed and sins forgiven, and to be freed from the power and slavery of sin. It doesn't take very long for a new Christian to come face to face with a surprising reality: the Christian is not done sinning. Sin has not given up on the Christian. In fact, the Christian will be increasingly aware of his own sin as he grows in Christ-likeness. When you come to Christ, you begin to realize that sin is not just the big, bad, dirty deeds that some people out there do somewhere; sin infects

---

7   Unbelievers can feel the pangs of *conscience*, which God has placed in every human heart. While the conscience is an onboard indicator that categories of right and wrong exist, it can be reprogrammed and ignored. Because of sin, the conscience is not a reliable guide to God's categorizations of sin.

the motives, the thoughts, the affections, and the actions that spring from them. Sin comes from who I am—my heart is the culprit, and my insides spill out in words and actions that displease God and hurt others.

A born-again person is really an odd creature, a citizen of two worlds, set apart by God, yet left here on the earth. He is forgiven of every sin he would ever commit, yet haunted by a resident evil. He is declared righteous by God, yet he perpetrates deeds of ungodliness. The cross-work of Jesus Christ has fundamentally altered his relationship to sin. The Christian has been forgiven sin's penalty (Romans 5:9), is no longer under the power of sin's dominion (Romans 5:21-6:23), and will one day be delivered from sin's presence (Romans 8:29-30). But because the presence of sin has not yet been eradicated, a civil war rages. A new palette of God-ward affections and a new ability to fight sin wages war against residual depravity. The Christian will fight because, for the first time, he can. How is a Christian supposed to fight this battle? He must fight on the foundation of the same gospel truth that purchased his pardon. John Owen said it this way: "Nothing but the death of Christ for us will be the death of sin in us."[8] The gospel of God's grace is the armory for all fighting against sin. Every attempt to fight sin without reference to the cross-work of Christ and dependence upon the power of the Holy Spirit will fail.

God's Word provides a variety of implements for waging war against sin. These implements are not opposed to truths of the gospel or the power of the Holy Spirit. Rather, the proper use of any of Scripture's weapons depends upon the cross-work of the Savior and the heart-work of the Holy Spirit. Memorizing Scripture (Psalm 119:11), taking drastic measures (Matthew 18:8), fleeing (1 Corinthians 6:18),

---

8 John Owen, *A Treatise of the Dominion of Sin and Grace* in vol. 7 of *The Works of John Owen*, ed. William H. Goold (Edinburgh: The Banner of Truth Trust, 2001), 529.

removing provision for the flesh (Romans 13:14), maintaining an employment in beneficial activity (1 Timothy 4:14-15), being encouraged by others (Hebrews 10:25-27), donning God's armor (Ephesians 6:10-16), and practicing church discipline (Matthew 18:15-17) are just some of the effective weapons with which God equips the believer for his fight against sin. All of these implements ought to be employed with eyes fixed on Jesus (Hebrews 12:1-2) and our hearts bolstered with the truth of our justification (Romans 8:1), and there is yet another tool worth brandishing: the implement called waiting on God.

Waiting on God is the theme of this book. How might the duty, the discipline, and the delight of waiting on God be enlisted in my fight with sin? How might God's Word direct us in this matter? What does it mean to wait on God in my fight with sin?

Failure to wait on God in the midst of temptation is the fruit of our innate desire for immediate gratification. We want what we want, and we want it now. We believe sin's lies, and we disbelieve God's truths. Giving in to temptation is at its root a failure of faith. I distrust God, believing that I know better what would satisfy the need of the moment.

Waiting on God in the midst of temptation is the triumph of faith. It means that I trust God, even when I do not understand my circumstance. I trust that God is better than whatever sin promises in the moment. I believe what He says about Himself, and I believe what He says about sin. To wait on God in the midst of temptation means to love God more than an immediate "gain." To wait on God is to suspend my own judgment, to surrender my assessment of my circumstance, and to entrust my heart and my life fully to His care. Fighting temptation is hard. I need help outside of myself. I need God.

Waiting on God in the midst of temptation requires self-shepherding.

I must learn to tell my heart, "Heart, you are deceived. God knows better than you do. Wait on Him." And then it requires waiting for God to provide. To provide what? We will see that God promises to provide us what is good, He promises a way of escape, He promises spiritual fruit, and He promises a final transformation. I offer you four waiting-on-God strategies for battling temptation, four tactics that enlist waiting as a weapon against sin as you stand on the solid ground of God's great promises.

Wait on God for What Is Good

The first strategy for fighting sin stands on a promise from God found in Psalm 84: God gives what is good. "For Yahweh God is a sun and shield; Yahweh gives grace and glory; no good thing does He withhold from those who walk uprightly. O Yahweh of hosts, how blessed is the man who trusts in You!" (Psalm 84:11–12). These are my own personal counseling verses. I have learned to speak these verses to my heart when I am tempted by sin. Verse 11 provides three essential truths about God, and verse 12 promises a blessing for trusting Him.

In the first line of verse 11, the psalm writer employs two metaphors to convey the first theological truth that we need to know. Yahweh God is a sun and a shield. The sun gives heat. A shield protects. The sun dominates the daytime sky, and all life depends on its energy. A shield blocks the weapons of an attacker, and a soldier is dependent on its cover. In calling God a sun and a shield, he is expressing his dependence upon God for life and safety. This perspective helps in a time of temptation.

Sin promises something bigger and better for us if we will run from the Sun and Shield, and yet nothing could be further from the truth. Humanity learned at the Garden of Eden that separation from

Yahweh means darkness and death. The psalmist reminds us that the only refuge in a sin-cursed and broken world is God, the sun and shield for those who hide themselves in Him.

The psalmist gives us a second needed truth in the second line of verse 11: Yahweh gives grace and glory. Grace is the undeserved favor, love, and kindness to people who don't deserve it. Glory is the full weightiness of God Himself given freely to His people. Grace and glory are too good to be true! How is it that undeserving rebels could gain access to the great Treasure of the universe, especially since He is the One whom we have so grievously offended by our sin? The promises of sin cannot compete with grace and glory! Sin at its best can only proffer cheap, evaporating thrills. Every promise that sin makes comes with strings—the unexpected consequences of slavery, destruction, and death. We never get what we bargained for when we make deals with temptation. Yahweh gives grace and glory. My heart needs to remember what Yahweh gives.

The third line of verse 11 contains a truth that has proved invaluable to me in my fight with sin: "No good thing does God withhold from those who walk uprightly." God describes His people here as "those who walk uprightly." They are not sinless, but they are characterized by orienting their lives according to God's ways. The truth is simple—our God is not in the business of withholding. Do you know that? Do you believe that God is not in the business of dangling good things over you only to keep them just out of reach? Yahweh overflows with kindness and compassion and goodness. He is good, and He does good, and He gives good to His own. He is like a father who gives good gifts to His children. God is not stingy.

When I was twenty-one years old, I was convinced that I was ready to be married. I believed I was the kind of man that would serve a wife well for the glory of God. I know now that would not have been good for any girl, and it would not have been good for me. I still had a lot to learn and a long way to grow. I believe marriage would have been a disaster for me at twenty-one. God does withhold things, but He never withholds the things that would be for our best and for His glory. He can withhold bad things, and He can withhold good things at bad times. You and I need to learn to wait on God for what is good when it is good. And we need to learn to trust God's judgment.

How many facts does your brain contain? Make a list of all of the facts that you possess. Write them all down. You know quite a bit. You have experienced a lot. Your knowledge is pretty extensive. Now consider all knowable facts. How many stars reside in our galaxy? In all of the galaxies? How many galaxies inhabit the universe? How many hairs grace your dome? For some of us that is a more approachable number than for others. How many of each kind of fish are swimming in the oceans right now? How many swam one year ago? How many fish swam in 1492? How many fish have there ever been? Consider all of their activities and all of their anatomical structures. Think of all the mysteries of chemistry and biology. Consider all of the facts of history. God knows what actually happened—every detail, every event, from all time. God knows the name and chemical composition of every star in every galaxy, and He knows each of us far more accurately than we perceive ourselves.

Who is smarter? Who is wiser? If you take any time to compare what you know with what God knows, you will repent in dust and ashes. I tend to give my finite, puny brain way too much credit in light of the vast resources of the knowledge of God. It is not just that we have less information than God, who has all the information; but we have wrong information. We have corrupt data, skewed interpretations, and wrong motivations. Now whom should we trust?

I have made plans for my life, and God's plans have always proven better. Learn to wait on God for what is good. "No good thing does He withhold from those who walk uprightly" (Psalm 84:11). Trust Him and take comfort in His character and provision. God's knowledge of your situation is perfect. His love for you is unflinching. His timing is perfect. Notice the faith exercised by the psalmist in verse 12: "Blessed is the man who trusts in You." You are blessed if you trust in Yahweh. Trust is a "waiting" word. You do not trust for things you already have. You trust the One who is good when you feel like you are missing something. How do you fight temptation when sin promises immediate gratification? Trust the One who is good. He is not stingy. He does not withhold good from those who walk with Him. Wait for Him.

Wait on God for a Way of Escape

I employ a second strategy for waiting on God in my fight with sin. It rests on God's promise of a way of escape. In I Corinthians 10:13 Paul writes, "No temptation has overtaken you but such as is common to man; and God is faithful, who will not allow you to be tempted beyond what you are able, but with the temptation will provide the way of escape also, so that you will be able to endure it."

I tend to believe that my temptation is unique to me, that I am the only one who has ever faced this. I believe the lie that there is no way out—the only road before me is to sin. Have you ever felt that way?

What does 1 Corinthians 10:13 teach us about temptations? They are not unique. This truth does not lessen the burden of a consuming temptation; it pulls the rug out from under the lie that this burden is too tough for God's prescriptions. Have you ever had someone try to comfort you by comparison to a tougher trial? "Hey, it's too bad that you can't find your keys, but at least you are not in a concentration camp." One-up-manship is not comforting counsel because it lacks empathy and fails to direct us God-ward. Genuine comfort is available in recognizing the universality of suffering in the human condition. Every temptation is a real burden, and it helps to have the perspective that no temptation is unique. You are not alone in it. Everybody suffers; everybody is tried; everyone faces temptation. Yours is common to man. There is nothing new under the sun, and God has already made provision for our need.

The grammar of verse 13 is striking. After a long statement about temptation, Paul gives a very short, arresting truth which ought to catch our attention: "God is faithful." It stands out. Paul wants to drive home the character of God. God keeps His promises.

It is tragic how quickly we trust ourselves and distrust God. I give myself reason every day to doubt myself, to mistrust myself, to disbelieve my own reasoning and motives. And yet who is the first person I turn to for insight when I am tried? Me. I distrust others, and I trust me. I distrust God, and I trust me. This irrational tendency ought to tell us something of the nature of our hearts and the way we think. "He who trusts in his own heart is a fool" (Proverbs 28:26).

God has never failed. God has never lied. He has never backed out of a promise. He has never made a commitment to us and then reneged on it because we didn't keep up our end of the bargain. He is faithful. Notice what His faithfulness to us produces. He will not allow you to be tempted beyond what you are able, and with the temptation He provides a way of escape.

This promise is vitally important: you will never be forced to bear more than you can. God knows and loves you as a son or daughter. He understands the operations of your heart, affections, and logic, and He has provided what you need for life and for godliness. By His grace in the gospel, new creatures in Christ have new affections, abilities, loves, and power. You are no longer a slave to sin; you are a slave to Christ, and God has a vested interest in you. He wants to display the power of His transforming work in you to a watching world. Even more, God Himself dwells in you by His Holy Spirit. Do you realize, in all the times that you have sinned as a believer, you have never been tempted beyond what you could bear? And you never will be. It is a guarantee from God.

There is a second guarantee in this verse. God always provides an escape hatch. "God will provide the way of escape also." Notice that God's provision of an escape is future with respect to the time of temptation. He *will* provide the way of escape. You don't necessarily know what that escape is in any given situation until you get there. But God has promised that you will never be put into a corner where your only options are sin, sin, or sin. There is always a way out. Do you believe this? Can you preach this to your heart the next time you are tempted? Can you wait on God? Where is the escape hatch? We must learn to bank on God's promise and seek the exit He provides.

Sometimes we have the wrong idea about sin and temptation. We think, if God didn't want me to sin, He would take away these desires. "God, I prayed that you would take away my sinful desires, but You haven't. You must just want me to sin." Have you ever thought that? This kind of thinking reveals a faulty expectation that God's plan is for me to never face temptation, and we should suspect such faulty expectations to come from our polluted hearts. I have not yet been fully sanctified, and when I sin, I sin because I want to sin. The residual sinfulness inside me still rears its ugly head. My own heart puts forward clever arguments to make sin seem like the right choice. We must learn to be suspicious of ourselves, remembering that God, on the other hand, is trustworthy. We must wait on Him for a way of escape.

Wait on God for Spiritual Fruit

A third strategy comes from Galatians 6 and is anchored in God's promise of spiritual fruit. The strategy is this: wait on God like a farmer for spiritual harvest. Paul writes to the Galatian believers: "Do not be deceived, God is not mocked; for whatever a man sows, this he will also reap. For the one who sows to his own flesh will from the flesh reap corruption, but the one who sows to the Spirit will from the Spirit reap eternal life. Let us not lose heart in doing good, for in due time we will reap if we do not grow weary" (Galatians 6:7-9).

Farmers are hard-working people, and they do a lot of waiting. The very nature of their work requires waiting. You cannot have a field full of corn in a moment. The ground must be prepared, seeds must be planted, young plants must be cared for, and mature produce must be harvested and processed. Not many of us would make good farmers. We have grown accustomed to a microwave world. But farmers work and wait in the real world. Some things take time and labor.

Paul uses the analogy of reaping and sowing in Galatians 6 to describe the Christian life. He begins in verse 7 by simply saying, "Do not be deceived, God is not mocked." Whatever he is about to say, if I am on the wrong side of this, I will have been deceived and I will be attempting to mock God. This is serious.

Paul lays down a straight-forward principle here: if you sow to the flesh, you will reap destruction; if you sow to the Spirit, you will reap life. Therefore, do not grow weary of doing good. You will reap in due time.

When we sow to the flesh, we will inevitably reap a harvest of destruction. The "flesh" Paul has in mind is the residual corrupt nature still a part of every Christian—the old man still active in our lives. Before we were in Christ, we were totally "old man"; we had only one nature. And now in Christ, next to the old nature inside us is a new nature provided by God, empowered by the Holy Spirit to pursue Christ. We are two-natured creatures. Paul says that when you sow to the flesh, to the old nature, you reap destruction. When a farmer plants wheat, he should not expect to harvest kumquats. He should expect wheat.

Have you seen this principle operating in your life? A sinful disposition is often the harvest of unchecked sinful thinking. Sinful words are the overflow of un-corralled sinful affections. Unbroken patterns of sin beget more sin. We often believe that a sin is an isolated event. "I will give in to this temptation this once, just a little bit. Surely it can have no bearing on my future. There will be no consequences in the hours, days, weeks, months, or years to come." That is one of the lies my sin nature loves to propagate. But God says, "Do not be deceived and do not mock Me. You reap what you sow."

By contrast, "the one who sows to the Spirit will from the Spirit reap eternal life" (verse 8). I do not believe Paul is talking about how to become a Christian here. Sowing to the Spirit characterizes Christian living. To some degree every genuine believer will sow to the Spirit and bear spiritual fruit. Spiritual fruit is the unavoidable result of the work of the Holy Spirit in a regenerate human. A fruitless Christian is an oxymoron. A genuine Christian will reap eternal life, and eternal life is not merely a destination. Eternal life is a quality of life that begins at conversion (John 3:36; 11:25-26). Spiritual beings sow to the Spirit and reap eternal life, culminating in the day when we are with Christ and never sin again.

A friend of mine, a farmer, summarized Paul's farming principle this way: "You can't be sowing in Satan's greenhouse and be praying for crop failure." Do you get it? Sowing to the flesh and expecting spiritual fruit is self-deception and mockery of God.

I planted winter grass last fall. I wanted the lush, deep-green rye carpet that grows so well during our Arizona "winter," and I wanted it now! I put the seeds down. When just a few shy blades sprouted, I worried that birds had eaten most of the grass seed, so I threw more seeds down. Wrong move. I should have waited. The grass just needed a little more time. The grass came up right when it was supposed to, but I had put down so much grass seed that whole sections of my yard choked themselves out. My impatience resulted in the death of my dream of an enviable yard.

Suppose instead of grass seed I had thrown down seeds for dandelions, clover, and crabgrass. In a matter of weeks I could have a mature weed garden in my front yard. After the neighbors complained, I could mow down those weeds and broadcast some grass seed. How effective would my efforts be? I think you know the answer—any new grass would struggle to survive in a forest of weeds that were merely trimmed instead of being uprooted.

What seems obvious for lawn maintenance gets lost when applied to heart maintenance. If you consistently seed the flesh, but hope that sprinkling a little bit of spirit-seed over the top will produce a lively spiritual crop, you deceive yourself and mock God. Have you wondered why your morning devotional won't break patterns of stubborn sin? Never mind that you spent all week sowing to the flesh.

The principle is straight-forward: sow to the flesh and reap destruction. Sow to the Spirit and reap life. The important key is found in verse 9: endurance. This is what Eugene Peterson called "a long obedience in the same direction." Listen to Paul's words: "Let us not lose heart in doing good, for"—and here is your waiting-on-God phrase—"in due time we will reap if we do not grow weary." In due time. Sow to the spirit and wait. This is God's plan. This is the way spiritual growth happens. This is the way fighting temptation works—you work and you wait like a farmer.

Perhaps you have wrestled with this question: "God, if You hate sin and You love me, why did You leave me here with a sin nature?" It would be easier if we were perfectly sanctified and never sinned again. Wouldn't that be a great testimony to the power of the gospel? But what if God were up to something? What if He knew exactly what He was doing? What if His plan was good, consistent with His character and His purposes? I don't know exactly why God left us in this mixed condition, but I do know that in my fight with sin, in my waiting on God, I learn some things. I have discovered the dastardly nature of sin now as a Christian better than I ever knew it before I believed. I know more of the heights and depths of what God did through His Son at the cross much better now than when I first believed. And in waiting on God, I have seen how God proves Himself faithful when sin proves itself foul. That doesn't make sin good. That does not make me want to sin. God's goodness and beauty shine brighter against the black backdrop of my own sin. Every Christian acquainted with the reality of who he is, rescued by the unfathomable love of God through Christ, will forever be humbled and awed by a God who would "make Him who had no sin to be sin on our behalf, so that we might become the righteousness of God in Him" (2 Corinthians 5:21).

Wait on God for Final Transformation

The Apostle John gives believers a fourth strategy for fighting sin. Like the previous three strategies, this one stands on the promises of God. Yet the realization of this promise will not occur in this life. John writes: "Beloved, now we are children of God, and it has not appeared as yet what we will be. We know that when He appears, we will be like Him, because we will see Him just as He is. And everyone who has this hope fixed on Him purifies himself, just as He is pure" (1 John 3:2-3). John's is the strategy of hope. The anticipation of seeing Jesus and being like Jesus purifies us.

John lived longer than the rest of the Apostles, writing this letter in the early 90's A.D. Eventually imprisoned alone on an island long after the others had been martyred, John had to wait the longest to behold again the one he walked with in Galilee. Do you think he awaited his home-going with eager anticipation? Longing for Christ and longing for Christ-likeness have a purifying effect on the soul.

John writes to Christians, calling them "beloved" and "children of God." Stop right there. Those are staggering declarations! God loves us! We have no business being in God's family, and yet here we are—not simply forgiven, but adopted—children of God! and loved! If you were to assess your own heart, your own life, your thought processes, and your motives by the light of Scripture, you might say, "Wow, I don't feel like a child of God; I don't always act like a child of God. I certainly love God, but I don't love Him well. I want to obey God, but I don't do that particularly well, either. I'm a child of God? Is this all there is to being God's child?"

This is not all there is. You, Christian, are absolutely and unequivocally God's child by His sovereign adoption. But you are not yet what you will be. More is coming. We know that when Jesus appears we will be like Him. We will be like Jesus as far as it is possible for humans to be like the Son of God, because we will see Him just as He is. Jesus is coming! And you get to be like Him! You will see Him as He is! He will no longer be cloaked; He will no longer be invisible. We are blessed in that we cling by faith to the One we have not seen, but a day is coming when we will see Him! He will no longer be shrouded in the ignominy of the incarnation. He will be uncloaked, the way the disciples saw Him on the mountain in Matthew 17, the way John saw Him in the first chapter of Revelation—so brilliant, so big, that humans fall on their faces.

What effect would regular anticipation of your future have on your fight with sin? Notice John's words: "Everyone who has this hope purifies himself just as [Jesus] is pure" (verse 3). Think about that. Can you simultaneously anticipate the return of Jesus and embrace the things that Jesus hates? Can you with the same breath long for your transformation and revel in the trash for which Jesus was crucified?

If your gaze is fixed on the anticipation of being with Jesus and being like Jesus, this hope will create something in your heart now as you fight against sin. Your affections will be calibrated to heaven's standards. Eagerly waiting for Jesus helps us to fight sin and temptation. It helps us put temptation on the timeline of eternity, to weigh it in the balance; and it helps us to set the compass of our affections true, to love what God loves and to hate what He hates.

One could state a logical corollary to this verse: the one not purifying himself evidently does not have this hope. If you are not actively fighting sin in your life, this is an indication that you do not possess this hope at all.

Don't Wait To Repent

You should not wait around for repentance. If you are not in Christ, "Today is the day of salvation" (2 Corinthians 6:2). You are not guaranteed one more breath on this earth. You will step out of time and into eternity to face a holy God who hates sin. This same God who hates sin loves sinners. He made provision for anyone who would come to Him for forgiveness through His Son. You can have new life, a conscience cleansed, sins forgiven, and a life with God.

If you are a Christian, but you are toying with "delayed repentance," beware! Waiting to repent is rebellion. This is dangerous territory. Sin wants to infiltrate and destroy, sinking its hooks in the heart and taking the life. Sin creates increasing cycles of temptation and sin. Delayed repentance sows the seeds of future hard-heartedness, leading eventually to apostasy. Do not wait to repent. Run away from sin's false advertising that promises stuff it cannot give, and turn to the One who is good and does good. He gives grace and glory. He is a sun and a shield; blessed is the man who trusts in Him.

WAITING ON GOD
FOR JUDGMENT

Between 1880 and 1891, a feud erupted between two families perched on either side of the Big Sandy River, separating West Virginia and Kentucky. The feud grew so fierce that the militia from both states were called in to intervene and to put a stop to the fighting. The rivalry between the McCoy and Hatfield families has become a modern parable on personal vengeance. The feud purportedly began when Asa Harmen McCoy was killed for fighting on the "wrong" side of the Civil War. One life was exchanged for another, vengeance was taken, McCoys were killed for Hatfields, and Hatfields were killed for McCoys. At one point, a fatal fight erupted over the possession of a pig. Whose pig was it? Apparently, the McCoys' branded pig marched itself onto the Hatfields' property.

"It's on our land, it's our pig."

"It's got our marking. It's our pig."

Gunshots. Dead people.

It did not end well. A dozen people were killed in cold blood, and at least ten were injured severely. Generations later, the story does have a happy ending. In 1979, the descendants of the Hatfields and McCoys hashed out their differences on the television game-show "Family Feud." A McCoy victory (the spoils: cash prizes and a pig) settled the long score.

What would life be like if the duty of meting out vengeance was ours? What would the world be like if justice was in our hands, if the vindication of wrong was left up to every individual? In William Golding's novel *Lord of the Flies*, a bunch of shipwrecked school kids wash up on an island. Stranded and fending for themselves, they create their own society. Before long jealousy over a seashell turns to rage, to murder, to vengeance. It is awful to contemplate what that would be like on a global scale. What if the Hatfield-McCoy feud spread to every family? Bloodshed. Retaliation. Re-retaliation. Anarchy.

Don't Take Vengeance

An essential component to waiting on God is the discipline of waiting for God to judge evil. It is wise to wait for God to exact justice. The fool demands ultimate justice before its time. Many passages of Scripture speak to this theme. I like Proverbs 20:22 because it is short and simple; there are not very many words. In fact, you could easily memorize it before you finish reading this chapter. In this proverb we listen in on God's wisdom through Solomon about what to do when people do us wrong. "Do not say, 'I will repay evil.' Wait for Yahweh and He will save you."

Three simple statements make up this proverb: a prohibition, a command, and a promise. The concepts are simple. The vocabulary is elementary. But living out this wisdom proves difficult. What goes on in your heart when someone sins against you? What do you feel? What would you do if you had the power to do it? What would common sense dictate? I fear our natural inclinations and gut reactions. The human race needs transcendent wisdom on this one, something that rises way above common sense. We need Divine guidance.

A Prohibition

Wisdom from God begins with a prohibition: "Do not say, 'I will repay evil.'" The word for "repay" is the Hebrew word "shalom," a concept freighted with significance. Used as a greeting, it conveys "hello," "goodbye," "peace," and "May it be well with you." The word has to do with peace, wellness, and wholeness. Shalom can refer to something that is complete or sound. In its verb form it means "to fulfill," "to restore," "to complete," or "to finish," as in the completion of the temple (I Kings 7:51), the restoration of years lost to locusts (Joel 2:25), the repayment of a debt (2 Kings 4:7), or the keeping of a vow (Deuteronomy 23).

Shalom came to designate recompense or payback. Good deeds could be rewarded. In I Samuel 24, David let Saul go free after Saul tried to kill him. Saul said to David, "may Yahweh **reward** you." The same word could be used not just for recompensing good deeds, but for recompensing bad deeds. In Isaiah 65:6, God said He would **repay** idolatrous Israel for her iniquities. And in Jeremiah 51:56, the same word is used: "Yahweh is a God of recompense. He will fully **repay**."

Shalom is not merely the absence of hostilities, but completeness, harmony, fulfillment, and unity. Shalom happens when things are set right, put in their proper order, and finished. Nearly two-thirds of the time shalom is spoken of in the Old Testament, it refers to a state of fulfillment or completeness as a result of God's presence. When God is present, things are made right. Consider the use of this word "shalom" in Isaiah 9, a familiar prophecy about Messiah's birth. Isaiah writes,

For a child will be born to us, a son will be given to us; and the government will rest on His shoulders; and His name will be called Wonderful Counselor, Mighty God, Eternal Father, Prince of **Peace**. There will be no end to the increase of His government or of **peace**, on the throne of David and over his kingdom, to establish it and to uphold it with justice and righteousness from then on and forevermore. The zeal of the Lord of hosts will accomplish this (Isaiah 9:6-7).

God Himself will come in the flesh to bring about shalom.

The idea behind "repay" in Proverbs 20:22 is of bringing parties together to harmonious completeness. God says to us, "Do not repay evil." Why this prohibition? When I am wronged, something needs to be done about it. Somebody clearly needs to do something, and that somebody is me. But God prohibits my natural inclination to bring "shalom" to the situation. Why aren't we to repay evil? Why can't we take justice into our own hands? The answers are really pretty obvious when we stop to thoughtfully ask the question.

You and I do not judge correctly. We have never actually interpreted anything with 100% accuracy. We are not omniscient. We misunderstand others' motives; we misjudge the intentions of our own hearts. Only God can see these. You and I have limited information, and we are blinded by our impulses and lusts. We are predisposed to promote self at the expense of others. We give ourselves the benefit of the doubt, while we assume the worst possible motives in others.

As evildoers ourselves, we really do not have a good grasp on what is evil and what is good. Our definitions of evil and good are skewed. Even in our redeemed state, we cannot shake the vestiges of fleshly thinking. We are not naturally given to thinking God's thoughts after

Him, and we do not see rightly as He sees. You are I are simply not qualified to mete out justice.

Even if we could assess a situation properly, we do not have the authority or the power to recompense evil. Even if we were impartial judges, we could not exact the recompense required for all parties to be made whole. We cannot create shalom because we cannot dispense the punishment appropriate for the crimes committed. Only God can bring shalom. George Lawson writes, "To say that we will recompense evil is the same as saying that we will step into the throne of God, wrest His thunderbolts out of His hands, and hurl them against all that we judge to be our enemies."[9]

Here is what God says: "Vengeance is mine, says the Lord. I will repay" (Romans 12:19). What a frightening thought that we, the ones deserving the vengeance of God, would attempt to usurp His role. Notice that God does not simply say, "Don't repay evil." His prohibition removes the taking of vengeance even from our talk. God instructs, "Do not say, 'I will repay evil.'" Even verbal threats are off-limits for us. Don't say it in your heart; don't let it pass your lips. Don't even let the thought cross your mind that you would pay back for evil. When people sin against us, God prohibits payback.

A Command

After the prohibition, God gives us a positive command: "Wait for Yahweh." Wait for the self-existent, covenant-keeping God of Israel. This is not like waiting for karma or for some inanimate idea of justice to run its course. We wait for a Person. We wait for our God. And what do we know about Him? He is just and good, and He does good. Omniscient and righteous, He judges without partiality. Why is it

---

9 George Lawson, *Proverbs* (Grand Rapids: Kregel Publications, 1984), 522.

God's solitary prerogative to repay evil? Consider sin's proportions. Sin against another finite sinner is awful, ugly, and bad. However, offense against an infinitely holy, good, beautiful, excellent, just, and right God is an offense of infinite proportions. This is a fundamental reason that you and I cannot repay evil. We do not begin to understand what sin is. We don't understand the proportions of what has been done or what is required in response. Only God comprehends the proportions of evil; therefore, only God executes vengeance.

A Promise

A promise follows the prohibition and the command, a promise from God for the final vindication of all injustice. The word "wait" in Proverbs 20:22 means to hope in something, to await with eager expectation, to patiently anticipate. Waiting is the ability to endure a situation under tension while your hope rests in Yahweh. Waiting for God to judge is an expression of faith. It is not easy to give up our grievances to the care of another. Charles Bridges said it well: "Revenge arises only because we have no faith. For did we believe that God would take up our cause, would we not leave ourselves implicitly in His hands?"[10] The Apostle Peter expressed this faith this way: "Therefore, those also who suffer according to the will of God shall entrust their souls to a faithful Creator in doing what is right" (1 Peter 4:19).

This is a fundamental expression of faith. This life is not going to go peachily all the time. So what do God's people do? They trust Him, and they wait. They entrust their souls to a faithful Creator. He is the one in charge of the entire universe, and He does not go back on His word. He is trustworthy, and He possesses the power and the resolve to do what is right on behalf of His people. He is our God.

---

10 Charles Bridges, *A Commentary on Proverbs* (Edinburgh: The Banner of Truth Trust, 1981), 355.

By indulging revenge, you and I do more harm to ourselves than our enemies ever could. No matter what an enemy may inflict upon us, "God causes all things to work together for our good" (Romans 8:28). He has destined us to be conformed to the image of His Son, and no adversary can thwart His good plan. Our enemies cannot take anything away from us, because everything that we truly possess is bound up in Christ, and it is unassailable. Our treasure has been purchased by His blood, and no moth can eat it, no rust can destroy it, no thief can come in and take it away. We have Him. The act of waiting places your concerns in the hands of someone who is competent, knowledgeable, powerful, and perfect.

Waiting on God for justice produces a dilemma: must all justice wait? God's temporary provision for a modicum of justice on the earth is the institution of human government. Human governments of all sorts are God's instruments to help us wait on Him. Virtually every form of government is better than anarchy. All human governments are bad to one degree or another, as Winston Churchill quipped, "Democracy is the worst form of government, except for all those other forms that have been tried from time to time."[11] Yet imperfect human governments are God's method of removing the sword of vengeance out of the hand of the offended individual and putting it in the hands of an institution (Romans 13:1-6). If humanity did not wait on God for temporal justice through government, or for final vindication on judgment day, this world would be a blood bath.

We, as offended individuals, never judge these things rightly. Our indictments are inaccurate, and the consequences we dish out are way out of proportion. Like the feud between the Hatfields and the McCoys, one offense leads to a greater retribution; retaliation increases

---

11 Churchill said this in an address to the House of Commons, November 11, 1947.

until the escalation is so great that nobody but the state militia or a 1970's television game show can compel a cessation of hostilities.

Wait for a Great White Throne

The greatest remedy to the temptation to take revenge is to meditate carefully on the awful, final judgment of God against the ungodly. The twentieth chapter of the book of Revelation contains the most serious, sobering, arresting 130 words[12] ever penned. I read these words for the first time when I was eight years old, and they have profoundly affected my life.

> Then I saw a great white throne and Him who sat upon it, from whose presence earth and heaven fled away, and no place was found for them. And I saw the dead, the great and the small, standing before the throne, and books were opened; and another book was opened, which is the book of life; and the dead were judged from the things which were written in the books, according to their deeds. And the sea gave up the dead which were in it, and death and Hades gave up the dead which were in them; and they were judged, every one of them according to their deeds. Then death and Hades were thrown into the lake of fire. This is the second death, the lake of fire. And if anyone's name was not found written in the book of life, he was thrown into the lake of fire (Revelation 20:11-15).

This is a difficult passage of Scripture, and not because of difficult words, cumbersome grammar, or complicated structure. This is a

---

12 There are 130 words in the Greek original, in case you counted a few more in your English Bible.

clear, straight-forward, easy-to-understand portion of your Bible. It is difficult because of what it so clearly says: God will judge the wicked by their deeds and consign them to eternal punishment.

Sustained reflection on this portion of Scripture turns my stomach to knots. This is not the passage of your Bible that you come to meditate on for comfort. We sneak up to the edge of it, take a peek, turn away, and shudder. This is a passage we approach with trembling, and we leave quickly. Yet we must come to grips with these words from God, for they depict the destination of every human being whose destiny has not been radically altered by Jesus Christ.

John the Apostle penned these words somewhere near AD 95 while imprisoned on the island of Patmos, the Alcatraz of the ancient Roman world. John was incarcerated on this bleak rock in the Mediterranean because of his love for Jesus and his proclamation of the gospel. There, awaiting the Savior on whose chest he had reclined during dinner some six decades prior, John recorded the future history of mankind. Near the end of this vision, John describes the great and final judgment of God against sin.

This is not the only end-times judgment depicted in the Bible. There are several, and they are not all the same. There will be a judgment of rewards for believers (1 Corinthians 3:10-15; 2 Corinthians 5:10). There will be a separation of believers and unbelievers at the end of the Great Tribulation prior to the inception of the Millennial Kingdom (Matthew 25:31-46). Finally, after the thousand-year reign of Messiah Jesus on the earth, God will judge the dead. This last judgment, called the Great White Throne judgment, has five features.

The Judge

"Then I saw a great white throne and Him who sat upon it, from whose presence earth and heaven fled away, and no place was found for them" (Revelation 20:11). The Judge appears on a throne. Notice each each word in the description of this throne: a great, white throne. Thrones are mentioned 30 times in the book of Revelation, but this is *a throne*, its indefiniteness indicating its uniqueness from previously described thrones. It is a *great* throne, dwarfing those who stand before it. This throne is intimidating, humbling, daunting. Its size is in keeping with its significance. This throne is *white*. The seat, like its occupant and the judgment to be issued from it, is bright, pure, sinless, and right.

Next, John describes the occupant of this throne. God sits on this judgment chair. Specifically, God the Son, Jesus. Jesus Christ is the judge seated on this great, white throne, perched to issue final judgment against sin. Jesus Himself said, "not even the Father judges anyone, but He has given all judgment to the Son" (John 5:22). Paul wrote, "for [God] has fixed a day in which He will judge the world in righteousness through a Man whom He has appointed, having furnished proof to all men by raising Him from the dead" (Acts 17:31), and "Christ Jesus... is to judge the living and the dead" (2 Timothy 4:1).

The Judge on this throne is the One who created everything, the One who became a baby at Bethlehem and walked the earth among us. He is the One who went to the cross and was Himself judged by God for sin—not for His own sin, but for the sins of those He came to save. It is Jesus who will judge. It is Jesus who will sit on this throne and set everything right. He is the one true God, holy, awesome, and unflinching.

"From [Jesus'] presence earth and heaven fled away, and no place was found for them." At this point history ends. The universe as we know it will dissolve. The physical universe will run like a fugitive away from the presence of the One who sits on this throne. Peter described this moment: "But by His word the present heavens and earth are being reserved for fire, kept for the day of judgment and destruction of ungodly men" (2 Peter 3:7). Jesus promised, "Heaven and earth will pass away, but My words will never pass away" (Matthew 24:35). The present universe will be destroyed to make way for the new heavens and new earth described in the last two chapters of Revelation.

For everyone standing before this throne, this will be the most discomforting moment experienced to this point. The physical universe has fled from the presence of this awful Person seated on this irresistible throne. There can be no comfort for those consigned to stand here. Everything that has been familiar and friendly has run away. They will be vulnerable, exposed as they have never been before.

What will it be like? What will it be like to stand before an unflinching Judge with nowhere to hide, nothing to lean against, and no place to run? Their hometowns have been incinerated. Their trophies and their toys have melted into nothing. Even the ground they stood upon, the trodden earth they thought would always be there, has abandoned them. The universe has left them alone to face the judgment of its Maker. Every human relationship they forged is now irrelevant. Every temporal enjoyment they experienced is now empty of its meaning. Every vain pursuit is now shown to be the vanity that it always was. What will it be like?

The Judged

The second feature of this great and awful judgment is the mass of humanity assembled for assessment. "And I saw the dead, the great and the small, standing before the throne" (Revelation 20:12). Who are these dead? These are the wicked dead from all of human history. They did not participate in the resurrection of the dead in Christ at the rapture (1 Corinthians 15) or the resurrection of Tribulation martyrs (Revelation 20:4-5). Yet this is a resurrection. Every man and woman will experience a resurrection, "some to everlasting life, and others to disgrace and everlasting contempt" (Daniel 12:2). Everyone standing before this judgment throne was dead and is now very much alive.

Notice the way the apostle describes this crowd: "the great and the small." The great people will be there—the popular and the powerful, the wealthy and the wise, the smart and the strong, athletes and actors, kings and commanders, the beautiful people, the exceptional people. There is no one who has enough clout to exempt himself from this judgment. No one has enough money to avoid this event. No one has the right family connection. All the great men and women of history are leveled at this judgment. This immense white throne is the great equalizer of mankind. God will be exalted and the proud will be brought low before Him.

The little people will be there too: the kid who always got picked last in sports, the underachievers, the losers and loners, the miserable and the oppressed, people who suffered hardship and poverty, slaves and servants, the chronically ill, the disadvantaged and disenfranchised. No one is too small to be overlooked by this judgment. Suffering in this life does not exempt anyone from punishment in the next life. No one is so insignificant as to be missed by this judgment. They stand for final judgment and sentencing before the One seated on the throne. They have nothing to show for themselves except what they have done.

"The sea gave up its dead" (Revelation 20:13). Many cultures in the ancient world speculated about what happens to those who die at sea. Greeks and Romans in the first century were no exception, placing great importance on burial in the ground. It was believed by many that a death at sea led to a wandering, ethereal, hopeless existence in the afterlife. Jesus' point in revealing this detail is to reinforce the reality that no mode of death can grant exemption from appearing at this judgment.

It matters not whether one's physical corpse pushes poppies or feeds the fish; all of the wicked dead will be brought physically to this event. The physical body of every individual will be reconstituted, reunited with his or her immaterial soul, and presented before this throne.

John gives further definitiveness to this resurrection: "Death and Hades gave up their dead" (Revelation 20:13). "Death" is the word depicting the separation of body from soul. Human beings are created material and immaterial, united in life, separated in death. "Hades" is the Greek word for the temporary abode of departed souls. When a wicked person dies, his physical body decomposes while his immaterial person—his inner self—arrives in Hades. Hades is a temporary place of torment under God's anger. At the final judgment, Death and Hades will give up their dead to this second resurrection. The immaterial person will be reunited with a reconstituted physical body in order to stand before Jesus for evaluation.

What will it be like? What will it be like to be raised from the dead? To be removed from Hades' torment and to be given a new physical body fit for eternal existence? To stand as a complete human being, immaterial and material united for the express purpose of facing this terrible day of reckoning? What will it be like?

The Evidence

The third feature of this Great White Throne Judgment is an irrefutable display of evidence. "And books were opened, and another book was opened, which is the book of life" (20:12). What are these books? These books are the evidence, in two parts. The first part is the record of wrongs. "And the dead were judged from the things which were written in the books, according to their deeds" (20:12). These books contain the record of every deed committed by every individual standing before God on that day.

No one will be able to say that the evidence was not properly gathered or processed. The evidence is complete and accurate. It has not been altered, exaggerated, diminished, or tampered with in any way. The evidence on display in these books comes from the infallible memory of an omnipresent, omniscient God! He has been everywhere and He has seen everything. No deed has escaped His eye. No careless word has missed His ear. No stray thought has eluded His perception. "All things are open and laid bare to the eyes of Him with whom we have to do" (Hebrews 4:13). Jeremiah writes, "'Can a man hide himself in hiding places so I do not see him?' declares Yahweh. 'Do I not fill the heavens and the earth?' declares Yahweh" (Jeremiah 23:24). Every man's closet will be emptied, and the skeletons will spill out for all to see.

The second part of the evidence is the registry of life. Called "another book," this is the book of life in which are written all the names of those who belong to Jesus. This second piece of evidence is especially deflating—nobody at this judgment has his name in the book of life. Their names are all over the other books. But this most important book, this Book of Mercy, does not contain their names.

The evidence is on display, and no mitigating circumstances can plead for leniency. Everything on record is a liability. Every piece of evidence is a smoking gun and a bloody glove. The unflinching truth of the evidence is a shock, given that people naturally prized their own accomplishments, underestimated their vices, concealed their dark motives, and masked their self-worship. They imagined that being "sincere" in their rebellion against their Maker was virtuous, that "authentic" treason had value. They imagined the final judgment to be some cosmic scale weighing "good" deeds against bad, and they imagined that God would overlook frailties in view of the surpassing value of sharing heaven with specimens as great as they. Such vain imaginations, themselves sinful manifestations of blind idolatry and antagonism toward their Judge, will not rescue them on that day.

What will it be like to hear books open? To know that there really never were any secrets? To understand for the first time that every "good deed" was trash. To have all of it irrefutably on display? What will it be like to be without remedy, without arbiter, without hope?

The Evaluation

The fourth feature of this Great White Throne judgment is a personal, accurate, and final evaluation. "And the dead were judged from the things which were written in the books, according to their deeds.... And they were judged, every one of them, according to their deeds" (Revelation 20:12-13).

God's final evaluation of humanity is personal. Notice how John expressed it: they were judged—a plural subject—the entire mass of unforgiven humanity is to be judged. And yet verse 13 reads, "every one of them." The verse literally states, "each one, they were judged." This awkward grammar accurately describes the scene. The corporate mass is evaluated individually. Jesus' judgment is personal. No one gets lost in the crowd.

This evaluation is not only personal, it is also accurate. God judges without partiality or favoritism. No consideration will be given for race, wealth, beauty, fame, earthly power, or family lineage. What are judged here are deeds—the things human beings actually did while alive on the earth—every action, every word, every thought, and every secret. God has warned us about this judgment for millennia. Through the apostle Paul, God told us that our actions would be evaluated: "Because of your stubbornness and unrepentant heart you are storing up wrath for yourself in the day of wrath and revelation of the righteous judgment of God, who will render to each person according to

115

his deeds" (Romans 2:5-6). Jesus indicated that our words would be evaluated: "But I tell you that every careless word that people speak, they shall give an accounting for it in the day of judgment" (Matthew 12:36). Our thoughts, too, have always been known by God: "Even before there is a word on my tongue, behold, O Yahweh, You know it all" (Psalm 139:4). Indeed, our deepest, darkest secrets have never really been kept to ourselves: "On the day when God will judge the secrets of men through Christ Jesus" (Romans 2:16). Listen to the words of Jeremiah 17:10—"I, Yahweh, search the heart, I test the mind, even to give to each man according to his ways, according to the results of his deeds."

Because God's evaluation will be accurate, His evaluation will result in degrees of punishment (Luke 12:47-48). Every human action will be shown for what it truly is. God's judgment will not be based on good intentions, primarily because sinful men and women do not have good intentions. Do you remember God's assessment of mankind in Genesis 6:5? "Every intention of the thoughts of his heart was only evil continually." We cannot be rescued by our "good intentions," for we lack them. Our evil actions spring from our evil hearts (Luke 6:45, Matthew 15:19), and the best we have to offer are offensive to God (Isaiah 64:6; Philippians 3:4-8).

God's evaluation of His enemies will be personal, accurate, and final. Every mouth will be silenced by the absolute rightness of this judgment. None will dare utter an excuse, blame-shift, or comparison. There will be no room for lawyers or jurors. The Judge is flawless, the evidence is immaculate, the evaluation is without error. There can be no appeal.

Skeptics of biblical truth have often complained about evil, demanding, "How can God be good when evil exists in the world?" Or even, "How can God exist when evil exists in the world?" Never mind that the perpetrators of evil, standing on God's green earth and breathing His oxygen, are the ones demanding justice. Such skeptics do not truly desire the eradication of evil; they wish for the extinction of God. The one who truly longs for the end of evil recognizes evil in his own heart, runs to God for remedy, and humbly waits for God to have His day. Rebellious perpetrators confuse God's mercy with impotence or license: "Because the sentence against an evil deed is not executed quickly, therefore the hearts of the sons of men among them are given fully to do evil" (Ecclesiastes 8:11).

Make no mistake; every cry for justice will be answered. God will deal with every evil. Every mass-murder, genocide, and ethnic cleansing will be fully repaid. All acts of abuse, enslavement, immorality, theft, and lying will be addressed and avenged. Unseen lust and hatred and bitterness and envy and impatience and slander will be exposed and condemned. Every evil thought, foul motive, and misplaced affection will be recompensed. Every failure to love God with entirety of heart, mind, and strength will be seen for the treason that it is. Failure to love others will be known and punished. Every skeptic who suppressed truth in unrighteousness (Romans 1:18-20) and every rebel who loved darkness rather than light (John 3:19-21) will be shamed by his foolishness (Psalm 14:1).

Consider the fact that every time someone crossed you, cheated you, spoke unkindly to you, slandered you, or insulted you, they committed a much greater crime than you could ever have realized. They have crossed their Maker, and He will have His vengeance. He will have His day. He will vindicate His name and His honor. He will repay every evil deed. God will, with perfect fairness and impartial evaluation, judge every evildoer for every evil done, and He will consign them to eternal punishment.

What will it be like? What will it be like to face an unflinching, irrefutable, thorough, accurate, personal, and final judgment of your sin? What will it be like to face the just and inevitable sentence for your crimes?

The Sentence

The fifth and final feature of this judgment is the sentence. No task remains for this divine tribunal but to sentence the guilty and commence their punishment. Jesus begins with death itself. "Death and Hades were thrown into the lake of fire" (Revelation 20:14). Here, Death and Hades are personified and tossed into the place of eternal torment. Death, the separation of body and soul, is called the "last enemy" (1 Corinthians 15:26). After this judgment, that separating enemy is never to be operative again (Revelation 21:4). Likewise, Hades, the temporary abode of disembodied spirits, will be done away with forever.

What is this lake of fire? This sea of torment corresponds to Gehenna, or hell, in the Bible. It is the place of eternal conscious torment by God. It is real, literal, unending, physical punishment under the infinite, unquenchable wrath of Almighty God. He prepared this lake for the devil and his angels (Matthew 25:41). It now becomes the eternal residence for all who did not repent of their rebellion against Him. "And if anyone's name was not found written in the book of life, he was thrown into the lake of fire" (Revelation 20:15). This is terrifying. It is just so final. Throughout the Bible, God has threatened to repay, and on this great day, He will do exactly as He has said. There will be no second chance. No purgatory. No annihilation. No reincarnation.

What will it be like? What will it be like for the unrepentant to understand fully that they were so consequentially wrong? They had hoped against hope that God would not really judge, or that maybe He didn't even exist. Perhaps they had wagered that their "righteousness" would be acceptable to Him, that He would forget or overlook their accumulated guilt, and that they would get into heaven on their merits. All such wishful thinking has now evaporated in the searing heat of accurate evaluation. Every layer of self-atoning whitewash has been stripped, and the rotting corpses of their self-generated morality have been revealed for what they always were. What will it be like to abandon all hope, knowing that their eternal destination is to face the unending fury of God's righteous wrath poured out against them for their crimes?

There Is Still Hope

If you are reading this book, there is still hope for you. You are breathing God's oxygen, and you still have time to repent. It has been appointed for man to die once, and then to face judgment (Hebrews 9:27). But until you breathe your last breath, you have opportunity to avoid the coming judgment. To contemplate the Great White Throne judgment properly is to gain a better understanding of another judgment that occurred on a cross on a hill outside of Jerusalem nearly two thousand years ago. You must look behind the scenes to see it. On its surface, the death of Jesus of Nazareth was the torture and execution of a petty popular religious renegade at the hands of the mighty Roman Empire. But what wasn't seen—what could not be seen—was the decisive event of all of history. This moment was the turning point in the timeline of the universe.

The same features of judgment observed at the Great White Throne in Revelation 20 are on display at the cross. There is a Judge—God the Father. "Yahweh was pleased to crush Him, putting Him to grief" (Isaiah 53:10). The one judged was the innocent One—Jesus.

He was oppressed and He was afflicted, yet He did not open His mouth; like a lamb that is led to slaughter, and like a sheep that is silent before its shearers, so He did not open His mouth. By oppression and judgment He was taken away; and as for His generation, who considered that He was cut off out of the land of the living for the transgression of my people, to whom the stroke was due? (Isaiah 53:7-8).

The evidence was the record of our evil deeds, the sins of all who would ever believe in Him. "[God] made Him who knew no sin to be sin on our behalf, so that we might become the righteousness of God in Him" (2 Corinthians 5:21). The evaluation at the cross is too awful and too wonderful to be true, simultaneously. The Innocent was counted guilty. The guilty was declared righteous! "For Christ also died for sins once for all, the just for the unjust, so that He might bring us to God" (1 Peter 3:18). The sentence was death. As the substitute at my execution, Jesus took the punishment that I deserved. He endured the full, infinite fury of the wrath of God against all my sin, and He exhausted that infinite wrath as only He could.

What was it like? What was it like for the perfect Son of God to dwell among His rebellious creatures, to be unrecognized, misunderstood, maligned, shunned, mocked, beaten, and killed? What was it like for the One who hates sin to become sin on our behalf? What was it like for Jesus to bear our sin in His body, to experience from His Father the infinite anger due for our wretched behavior? He wrapped Himself in our vileness so that He could clothe us with His perfection.

For all who are in Jesus, scarlet stains have been made white as snow. Sins have been removed as far as east is from west. Iniquities have been taken away, forgiven, punished, paid for, and erased. Sinners have been acquitted, adopted, purchased, loved, set apart, rescued, reconciled, and declared righteous. We have been transferred from a dominion of death, darkness, and depravity to kingdom of life, light, and beauty. Jesus promised this transfer to anyone who would believe: "Truly, truly, I say to you, he who hears My word, and believes Him who sent Me, has eternal life, and does not come into judgment, but has passed out of death into life" (John 5:24). Jesus, the One who will judge, offers forgiveness, life, rescue, escape. He offers you Himself, and your name written in the book of life! Flee to Him while you still have breath.

Waiting on God to Set Things Right

God will set everything right. Do not say, "I will repay evil." Wait on God; He will repay. At the last judgment, Jesus will right every wrong and punish every offense. Do you believe this? The reality of final judgment ought to sober our response to the sins of others. The next time someone sins against you, slowly contemplate the scene in Revelation 20. Think carefully about what it will be like for the person who offended you to face the omnipotent, unflinching Judge of all. Your offender will face unmitigated fury for all of eternity (and if your offender is a Christian, then Jesus has already borne the awful punishment for that infraction). Ought we usurp God's role? The vindication of wrongs committed by others is not our task! Ours is not the infinitely offended nature. God is immeasurably more wronged by wrongdoing than we could ever be. We are sinners meriting judgment. Anything that we receive other than eternal hell is the mercy of God toward the undeserving.

Waiting on God means, in part, setting aside our desire to mete out retribution. Waiting on God when we are wronged by others means trusting God's righteous assessment and His perfect timing. The contemplation of hell ought to produce compassion toward sinners and thankfulness for our own rescue. I am convinced that we do not think of hell often enough. If our hearts were regularly saturated with the awfulness of coming judgment, we would be far less concerned with how we have been offended, and far more concerned to preach the gospel to offenders rushing headlong into eternal punishment. Maintaining a correct perspective on coming judgment will fuel our compassion for others and our faith in God's plan as we wait for Him to make all things right.

DON'T WAIT

Not all waiting is good. Waiting 'for the other shoe to drop' is an alias for sinful worry. Waiting to obey is disobedience. And waiting to repent is rebellion. I have a fear, grounded in my own experience, that I could employ the biblical concept of waiting on God to mask laziness, sloth, and a lack of discipline. My flesh loves theological camouflage. A biblically-informed sin nature is apt to re-label procrastination as trust in order to evade culpability. Who can accuse me of being lazy if I am "waiting on the Lord"?

A man who needs a job to provide for his household may claim to be trusting the Lord for employment while he sits on his couch with a television remote. I would hate for anyone reading this book about waiting on God to equip his flesh with a theological camouflage for laziness. Putting lipstick on the sloth neither provides for my family nor fools God.

This chapter seeks to develop a biblical work ethic. Hard work and diligent labor do not oppose waiting on God. Waiting on God is a disposition that produces trusting obedience. If the task at hand is to find employment, and "waiting on the Lord" is an excuse for failing to construct a resume and turn in applications, something is wrong. If the task at hand is to be holy, and I say, "I'm waiting on the Lord for holiness," but I'm not diligently applying the Christian disciplines (2 Peter 1:5), something is seriously amiss. If the task at hand is the Great Commission (Matthew 28:19), but we neglect preaching the gospel in our spheres and to the ends of the earth, we have misunderstood God.

America in the last few decades has experienced a seismic cultural shift. This once was the land of opportunity. It has become the land of entitlement. Once upon a time, a young man or woman looked out on a field of opportunities that rewarded imagination and diligent labor, longing for the opportunity to put their hands to the plow and make something for themselves. Today, we are taught that if somebody else has achieved what we desire, then we are entitled to what they have, but without doing what they did to get it. This subtle, but significant, shift in thinking will inevitably dismantle the economy and the culture that we have enjoyed. Yet far more deleterious than the effects on our way of living are the effects on our way of thinking. The craving of rewards without labor is a lust that leads to theft. The entitlement mentality that pervades today's culture is an envious and crude laziness.

Like the proverbial frog in the kettle, who does not sense the increasing water temperature until he is boiled alive, Christians are in danger of acquiescing to the entitlement psychology of the world around us. So as not to be conformed to the pattern of this world (Romans 12:2), we need to develop (or rediscover!) a countercultural work-ethic, a work-ethic whose origin and terminus are God Himself. The Christian ought to approach work like the rest of life, as worship. Rather than self-generated and self-glorifying, godly work draws deeply on the resources provided by God's grace, dependent on the power of the Holy Spirit, obeying God and waiting on God simultaneously. God-honoring work does what needs to be done when it needs to be done, trusting God with the results.

What follows is a biblical work ethic developed from two sources. The timeless wisdom of Proverbs constitutes the first, and the New Testament provides the second.

Developing a Work-Ethic from the Book of Proverbs

The book of Proverbs prepared God's people to prosper and to please God through hard work. God gave Solomon and his colleagues truisms for wise living under God's rule, providing His people with insight into how to experience joy and prosperity in life. While we as New Testament followers of Jesus do not live under Israel's theocracy, we too can live well and please God by the application of these Proverbs to our own work-ethic, summarized in the following eleven principles:

1. Marvel at the Foolishness of Laziness

"Foolishness" in the book of Proverbs does not describe the cute silliness of a clown, or the innocent naiveté of a friend just a little slow on the uptake (see Proverbs 17:12). "Fool" is a heavy-duty word designating a hell-bound rebel, antagonistic towards God, doing what he should not, and refusing to do what he ought. His naiveté is culpable and his rebellion is prosecutable. Foolishness in Proverbs is a defining sin needing repentance and correction. In order to please God in our work-ethic, we need to be appalled at the foolishness bound up in laziness. Observe these Proverbs:

"The sluggard does not plow after the autumn, so he begs during the harvest and has nothing" (Proverbs 20:4). The fool should have plowed when he could plow, and then he would have food to eat. But he didn't and now he doesn't. The wise man does what he should do when he should do it, while the lazy fool starves.

"The desire of the sluggard puts him to death, for his hands refuse to work; all day long he is craving" (Proverbs 21:25-26). What good is desire and craving without the action required for the fulfillment of desire? The old adage stands: "if wishes were horses, then beggars would ride." Desire is useless apart from the work that it takes to get something done.

> I passed by the field of the sluggard and by the vineyard of the man lacking sense, and behold, it was completely over-grown with thistles; its surface was covered with nettles, and its stone wall was broken down. When I saw, I reflected upon it; I looked, and received instruction. 'A little sleep, a little slumber, a little folding of the hands to rest,' then your poverty will come as a robber and your want like an armed man (Proverbs 24:30-34).

Destitution surprises the lazy fool. "Where did this poverty come from? Why is hunger at the door with a gun? Just because I didn't plow my field or pull the weeds?" The fool does not see the connection!

"The sluggard is wiser in his own eyes than seven men who can give a discreet answer" (Proverbs 26:13, 16). How foolish is this foolishness of laziness? So foolish that the fool thinks he is wise.

2. Detect The Disguises of Laziness

Laziness camouflages itself with less odious labels. We don't want to be called "lazy"—we just procrastinate. Learning to see through these euphemisms will help us build a God-honoring work-ethic:

Procrastination. Procrastination is a failure to do what you should do when you should do it. Procrastinators leave essential duties for later, preferring more enjoyable tasks now, hoping to pull off the buzzer-beater finish in miracle fashion. This is a form of laziness against which the Bible warns us: "Prepare your work outside and make it ready for yourself in the field; afterwards, then, build your house" (Proverbs 24:27). The wise man plants his fields before he decorates his home. Life is a series of prioritizations, and the lazy man (the fool) does what he wants to do before he does what he needs to do. God's wisdom is to do the necessary things first. Don't be fooled: one can be lazy and busy simultaneously. The procrastinator has perfected the art of being very busy doing everything except the one thing that needs to get done.

Haste. Your dad (or maybe your grandfather) said it to you an unbearable number of times: "Haste makes waste." He stole that from Proverbs 21:5, "The plans of the diligent lead surely to advantage, but everyone who is hasty comes surely to poverty." Rushing through tasks has the appearance of hard work, but it is another form of laziness. The man who is hasty in his work has not learned to worship God in the task, but is rather bent on flying through it to get to what he really wants to do. This kind of laziness precipitates poor products and poor people.

Distraction. Being easily distracted is another form of laziness. Proverbs 28:19 addresses the ADD in all of us: "He who tills his land will have plenty of food, but he who follows empty pursuits will have poverty in plenty." There is a time to work and a time to play, but the eyes of the lazy man are caught by recreation out-of-season. God's wisdom is to put your hand to the plow and do the work. Then there will be food to eat and time to play.

Cutting corners. "Cheat to win" and "Work smarter, not harder" are ready adages for the lazy. The wise man knows that "Wealth obtained by fraud dwindles, But the one who gathers by labor increases it" (Proverbs 13:11). Gains made by shortcut are often lost in the outcome. Did you read *Cliff's Notes* in high school? That is not the same as reading the book. Good teachers make lazy students pay at exam time, asking questions Cliff doesn't answer. Cutting corners is laziness, a dishonor to God and a discredit to a man.

Talking. Conversing about working is a convincing disguise for laziness. At least, the one doing the talking is convinced. "In all labor there is profit, But mere talk leads only to poverty" (Proverbs 14:23). Talking about getting a job is not the same thing as getting a job. When you don't have a full-time job and you need a full-time job, your full-time job is getting a full-time job. Talking about working brings home no bacon. Talking about serving others is not the same as serving others. Talking about praying is not the same as praying.

Thinking. Thinking things through is good, but thinking can be a disguise for laziness. Some people paralyze themselves through fear of every conceivable outcome to every possible contingency. Others camouflage their laziness with analysis. Ten things that could be done overwhelm the one thing that must be done. "The sluggard says, 'There is a lion in the road! A lion is in the open square!'" (Proverbs 26:13). The lazy man in this proverb needs to work, but is paralyzed by the analysis of some contingency. Waiting for the situation to be perfect before doing what must be done is not the same as waiting on God. Such waiting may actually reveal a failure to trust God through obedience.

Getting rich quickly. Proverbs 12:11 tells us, "He who tills his land will have plenty of bread, but he who pursues worthless things lacks sense." The get-rich-quick scheme promises a way to get what diligence produces, but without the hard work. Every day some fool falls for the windfall-promise of the get-rich-quick scheme. And every day someone regrets having fallen for it. The lazy man, hoping to cheat the diligence-produces-plenty-principle, lost time and precious resources chasing emptiness. A study of lottery winners will reveal a trail of depressing biographies that should make sane persons do anything they can to not win unearned money. The pursuit of quick wealth reveals an internal corruption and ends in self-destruction. "A man with an evil eye hastens after wealth and does not know that want will come upon him" (Proverbs 28:22). Incidentally, wealth is not the bogeyman. According to this proverb, having wealth is good and being in want is bad; but what produces want is the hastening after wealth, in contrast to the diligent pursuit of wealth through labor. Wealth cannot be your god, but it can be good. Longing for quick riches only brings poverty.

3. Understand the Results of Laziness

While laziness makes promises about short-term comfort and leisure, it inevitably leads to ruin. The effects of laziness are easy to see in the rear-view mirror and in the lives of others, but they are more difficult to take into account personally when a nap seems so inviting. The writers of Proverbs warn us about the manifold results of life lived lazily:

Poverty. Laziness produces poverty. Apparently an ant, with only 250,000 brain cells (compare that to 100 billion nerve cells alone in the human brain), knows much more about the value of hard work than we do.

"Go to the ant, O sluggard, observe her ways and be wise, which, having no chief, officer or ruler, prepares her food in the summer and gathers her provision in the harvest. How long will you lie down, o sluggard? When will you arise from your sleep? 'A little sleep, a little slumber, a little folding of the hands to rest'—Your poverty will come in like a vagabond and your need like an armed man" (Proverbs 6:6-11).

"Poor is he who works with a negligent hand, but the hand of the diligent makes rich" (Proverbs 10:4).

Shame. "He who gathers in summer is a son who acts wisely, but he who sleeps in harvest is a son who acts shamefully" (Proverbs 10:5). Sleeping during the harvest is a poignant example of laziness, bringing shame to a family. A person, or a culture, that has simultaneously lost its sense of shame and its work ethic is in for trouble.

Forced labor. Laziness narrows options. A grumbling stomach will induce even a sloth to labor, but he will not be free to work where he wants. "The hand of the diligent will rule, But the slack hand will be put to forced labor" (Proverbs 12:24). Hard workers increase the possibility of working on their own terms, setting their schedules, determining their pay, and selecting their coworkers.

Hunger. "The soul of the sluggard craves and gets nothing" (Proverbs 13:4). The lazy man owes his growling stomach to his lack of diligence.

Destruction. Far from being a passive peccadillo, laziness is an active malevolence, affecting many others beside the man who will not work. "He also who is slack in his work is brother to him who destroys" (Proverbs 18:9). If you want to walk arm in arm with destruction, be a lazy man.

4. Turn from Laziness Wherever you Find It

It is one thing to recognize laziness and its harmful results; it is another thing altogether to turn away from it. God has graciously given His people two tutors to steer us from the inevitable disasters which laziness brings. His Word is our first teacher, warning, commanding, and pleading with us to turn away from laziness. When fools refuse the kindness of His reliable Instructor, the substitute teacher is called in, namely, the consequences of our laziness. Listen to God's gracious warnings of the consequences in store for those who let the seeds of sloth grow to bear fruit. "Do not love sleep, or you will become poor; Open your eyes, and you will be satisfied with food" (Proverbs 20:13).

"Know well the condition of your flocks, and pay attention to your herds; for riches are not forever" (Proverbs 27:23). If you have plenty now, you cannot assume you'll have it tomorrow. A season of diligence may provide an opportunity to be tempted by laziness, but the reality is that yesterday's labors do not necessarily secure tomorrow's dinner. In order to have what you will need tomorrow, you must labor today.

Laziness narrows future possibilities, while diligence opens many doors. Consider what would happen to you if you lost your job today. If you have worked hard and saved money, you have options. Your resume reflects faithfulness, you have time to make a good decision about your next employment, and you will not starve or go into debt while you seek a new job. On the other hand, if you have been lazy and you lose your job, you are left with no job, a bad resume, and no savings. Your options are slim. Laziness closes doors of opportunity and opens the gate to disaster.

Laziness is not a personality trait; it is sin. Laziness is a failure to worship God in the tasks that are given to us. Sluggards in the workplace, at school, in the church, and at home do not please God. Laziness in your pursuit of Christ does not please God. Laziness is an enemy resident within us that must be thwarted.

5. Stay Away from Lazy People

It is not enough to fight only the laziness within us. God also warns us about the dangers of associations with lazy people. "Like vinegar to the teeth and smoke to the eyes, so is the lazy one to those who send him" (Proverbs 10:26). A lazy barista in a morning-rushed coffee shop is an irritation to a crowd of customers. "The way of the lazy is as a hedge of thorns, but the path of the upright is a highway" (Proverbs 15:19). The lazy man makes the road difficult, both for himself and for anyone else in his path. "He also who is slack in his work is brother to him who destroys" (Proverbs 18:9). If you want trouble, hire a sluggard.

I recently asked some Christian business owners what they thought about hiring Christians. Initially, these businessmen believed that a professing follower of Jesus would be characterized by integrity, loyalty, and diligence, and a Christian's application went to the top of the stack. They should be the most conscientious workers, because they will treat their tasks as worship. They will recognize that they truly work for Jesus, and they will want to please Him by working well, since they know they are accountable to God's Word for this perspective. But it did not take long for these business owners' perspectives to change. Applications that bore professions of faith in Jesus were more easily set aside, because professing Christians often do not make good employees. Why? According to these business owners, Christian employees are characteristically lazy. They expect more time off, and they expect to be excused when they show up late for work because they were "sharing the gospel with somebody." They expect benefits from Christian employers that other people don't get because they work for a Christian boss. Christians can be intolerant of others in the workplace, expecting non-Christians to behave like Christians, while at the same time being lazy on the job. They spend their time doing "spiritual" things and not the spiritual thing on the job which is the job. A prudent man avoids such characters.

6. Value the Results of Hard Work

Work is, in many respects, its own reward. Idleness, on the other hand, is a sinkhole ready to devour a life. Yet aside from the benefit of simply keeping a man out of trouble, diligent labor promises wealth (10:4), plenty (12:11), success (12:14), leadership (12:24), fulfilled goals (13:4), profit (14:23), and honor (22:29). These rewards are promised to the one who labors. "Where no oxen are, the manger is clean, but much revenue comes by the strength of the ox" (Proverbs 14:4). This proverb presents an intriguing contrast. You can have a clean stable or much revenue. It is a lot less work keeping the stable clean if you don't have oxen in it—no tidying up the food trough, no cleaning up at the other end. A stable would certainly smell nicer without all those animals. But without the animals, there is no revenue. It might be easier, but there's no profit in it. Abundance comes by the strength of the ox, which means you're going to have to get your hands dirty.

7. Learn to Do the Hard Thing First

"Prepare your work outside and make it ready for yourself in the field; afterwards, then, build your house" (Proverbs 24:27). Often the more difficult and less desirable task is the most necessary. How good are you at doing the hard thing first? Don't put off working on your left-handed layups just because you feel more comfortable at the free-throw line. Do the hard thing first. I enjoy mowing the lawn. It's easier for me to go push a lawn mower than to do other, more necessary, things. In the Christian disciplines, it is easier for me to read than to pray. We must learn the discipline of doing hard things first.

8. Finish What You Start

How many good books sit on your shelf half-read? There is no biblical command to read every book (and its footnotes) all the way to the end. But are you the kind of person that follows through, faithful in the details, to the end of the task? "A lazy man does not roast his prey" (Proverbs 12:27a). The lazy man in this proverb is not interested in starting a new wild-game-sushi fad. He is a fool who fails to finish the task at hand, and he goes hungry as a result. The lazy man in this proverb has done a lot of work—he has hunted and killed an animal, but the meat will rot because he has not taken the final steps of cooking his prize. He will not receive the reward of his initial labors because he failed to finish what he started. Laziness leaves much labor unrewarded.

9. Aspire to Be Diligent

The proverb continues with a contrast: "but the precious possession of a man is diligence" (Proverbs 12:27b). While the lazy man starves because he fails to finish, the godly man has a weapon in his arsenal far better than all the tools of the hunt that a lazy man could own. The godly man's diligence will see a task through to the end, and his hard work will reap the reward. The wise man values diligence as a precious possession. William Carey was the British pioneer missionary who, at the end of the 18th century, traveled to India and Bengal to take the Gospel to people who had never heard, translating the Bible, or portions of the Bible, into 35 different languages. Claiming to have few abilities, he said "I can plod and persevere. That is my only genius.

I can persevere in any definite pursuit. To this I owe everything."[13] We must aspire to diligence as the ordinary path to advancement.

10. Don't Rush

"The plans of the diligent lead surely to advantage, but everyone who is hasty comes surely to poverty" (Proverbs 21:5). Do you remember the race between the tortoise and the hare? The hare sprinted, stopped, ate carrots, read a book, took a nap—and the tortoise just kept walking and won the race. Whether or not the account is historically accurate, it serves to illustrate this proverb. Perhaps you heard your dad say, "Measure twice, cut once." Every time I make a return trip to the hardware store because I mis-cut a board, I can hear my dad's voice rehearsing this mantra. Don't train yourself to do quick, half-baked, regrettable work. Contrary to popular opinion, practice doesn't always make perfect. Practice makes permanent. Doing hasty, shoddy work trains you to do more hasty, shoddy work.

11. Work Theologically

If we are to build a biblical work-ethic from Proverbs, we must orient our work theologically. "Commit your works to Yahweh and your plans will be established" (Proverbs 16:3). Everything we do is to be done for the Lord, in dependence upon the Lord, as worship. We are to put in a good day's work, not for our glory, but for His; and not by our strength, but by His; and not for our benefit, but for our employer's benefit and the benefit of the people that we serve.

The workplace is to be no less "sacred" than the Sunday-morning service. The rescue of this biblical conviction was one of John Calvin's great gifts to western civilization. In Calvin's day, the priestly class in

---

13 S. Pearce Carey, *William Carey* (London: The Wakeman Trust, 1993), 20.

the church did "spiritual" things, while the laborers in the workplace did "secular" things. Worship took place in the church at the hands of the clergy, and the rest of society plodded through the mundane muck of merely physical existence. John Calvin set western civilization free by recovering the biblical truth that all of life is to be worship, including work.

Developing a Work-Ethic from the New Testament

A fuller theology of work-as-worship emerges in the New Testament. Here are several New Testament passages to consider as you think about what it means to labor for the glory of God.

1. The Why and How of Working for the Man

> Slaves, in all things obey those who are your masters on earth, not with external service, as those who merely please men, but with sincerity of heart, fearing the Lord. Whatever you do, do your work heartily, as for the Lord rather than for men, knowing that from the Lord you will receive the reward of the inheritance. It is the Lord Christ whom you serve (Colossians 3:22-24).

While today's workplace is not the slave-based economy of ancient Rome, the 21st-century Christian can glean important workplace principles by answering three basic questions addressed by this passage: Why do I work? How should I work? For whom do I work? According to Colossians 3:22, when you go to work, you are actually working for your employer. Even if you own your own business, you are working for others—your customers. Your efforts should benefit your employer, the employees, the company, and its customers. Additionally, according to verse 23, you are working for Jesus. You are serving the Lord Christ when you make widgets or trim hedges. How should you work? Not with "eye service," only doing what's expected of you when somebody is watching. And not as man-pleasers, working only to make the employer happy; no, you are to work to make your other boss happy, too, and that's Jesus. Your labor ought to be an outward expression of your inward worship of Christ, not with mere outward diligence, but as verse 23 says, "from the soul." Finally, why do you work, according to Colossians 3:24? You work for your reward, but the reward Paul has in mind is a bit farther down the road than your two-week check or your 401k. "From the Lord you will receive the reward of the inheritance." Did you know that you will be getting paid, by God in the eternal state, for your work at your temporal employment? Do a good job, because you are working for Him, and He will reward you. Verse 24 gives us another reason for our diligent labor in the workplace: "It is the Lord Christ whom you serve." If you make shoes or sell insurance as worship to Jesus, it is His work that you do, for His purposes and for His glory.

2. Labor for One Another in the Church

If you are to build a biblical work ethic, you can't stop when you punch out at the time-clock. The Christian is to labor in the church as well. Observe Paul's delineation of our responsibilities in the body of Christ:

Let love be without hypocrisy. Abhor what is evil; cling to what is good. Be devoted to one another in brotherly love; give preference to one another in honor; not lagging behind in diligence, fervent in spirit, serving the Lord; rejoicing in hope, persevering in tribulation, devoted to prayer, contributing to the needs of the saints, practicing hospitality (Romans 12:9-13).

This list of commands demands urgency, perseverance, devotion, diligence, and fervency.

3. Invest Your Talents

The punchline of Jesus' Parable of the Talents is "For to everyone who has, more shall be given, and he will have an abundance; but from the one who does not have, even what he does have shall be taken away" (Matthew 25:29). In this parable, Jesus portrays the eternal value of opportunities, abilities, time, resources, intelligence, talents, and relationships. He represents them as money, denominated in talents, divided between servants by a master going away on a journey. One servant was given five talents, another two, and another one. The master expected his servants not merely to avoid losing his money, but to gain more with it. The slave who merely returned his master's money, deemed wicked and lazy, was to be thrown out. Those who made more with what they had been given were rewarded with more still.

The Greek word *talent*, a measurement of money by weight, has entered the English language (probably from this parable!) to refer metaphorically to abilities or gifting, what we think of as "talents." Your abilities, opportunities, time, intelligence, resources, and relationships are a stewardship from your Master, who will render judgment and reward based on your dealings with His stuff. He gave you what you have; what are you doing with it?

4. Be Diligent in Your Affections for God

Jesus personally audited seven churches near the end of the first century. The Apostle John recorded these audits in Revelation 2-3, and the last church audited received this stern warning: "So because you are lukewarm, and neither hot nor cold, I will spit you out of

My mouth" (Revelation 3:16). The church at Laodicea resembled the water that supplied its city: lukewarm. Neither rejuvenating hot springs nor cool, invigorating fresh water were available to the city's residents, the city's water being supplied long distance through pipes. By the time any water reached Laodicea, it was insipid and unpalatable, often inducing sickness among the city's residents. The affections of the church that called Laodicea home were likewise tepid. Jesus' warning to the church was this: if you are lukewarm in your affections for God, you run the risk of being rejected by Him. Are you lazy, or are you laboring to cultivate your affections for God?

5. The World is Watching. How Are You Working?

Paul instructed the Thessalonians that their workplace diligence affected their gospel witness. "Make it your ambition to lead a quiet life and attend to your own business and work with your hands, just as we commanded you, so that you will behave properly toward outsiders and not be in any need" (1 Thessalonians 4:11-12). This sounds a lot like a work-ethic built on the wisdom of Proverbs, except that here the gospel is at stake. How a Christian works can either endorse or bring shame to the gospel. Watch how you work. The world is watching.

6. Don't Be a Mooch

Paul gave further instruction about work to the Christians at Thessalonica.

"For even when we were with you, we used to give you this order: if anyone is not willing to work, then he is not to eat, either. For we hear that some among you are leading an undisciplined life, doing no work at all, but acting like busybodies. Now such persons we command and exhort in the Lord Jesus Christ to work in quiet fashion and eat their own bread. But as for you, brethren, do not grow weary of doing good" (2 Thessalonians 3:10-13).

Mooching off of others is bad. Living off of others is a conglomeration of theft, unkindness, and lack of love. The opposite of mooching is labor and generosity, working hard with your own hands so that you have enough to give to others.

Hunger is supposed to be the real life consequence of laziness. If you don't work, according to Paul, you don't eat. We do not necessarily feel the sting of this in our day of safety nets and government assistance. Somebody is going to take care of you. The mooch may lean on brothers and sisters in Christ until he wears out his welcome and has to make new friends. There may be a string of relationships in your life that are broken because you've been taking, rather than working hard and giving. Notice what Paul says of the lazy Thessalonian believers: "we hear that some of you live a lazy life." Laziness gets noticed. Their work ethic spoke on their behalf. And they have not simply failed to get a job; they are living "undisciplined" lives. Laziness in one area usually shows up in other areas. "I don't want to work on my left-handed layups" easily translates into "I don't want to study" and "I don't want to take out the trash" and "I don't want to fight sin." Observe that Paul calls these lazy moochers "busybodies." Lazy people can be very busy, engaged in a whirlwind of unproductive activity. Paul's remedy is a specific command followed by a broad directive: work quietly, eating your own bread, and do not grow weary of doing good.

7. The Marathoner's Ethic

The Christian life is a race. But if this race is to be finished, it cannot be run at a dead sprint. We must learn to rest to run long. "Therefore, since we have so great a cloud of witnesses surrounding us, let us also lay aside every encumbrance and the sin which so easily entangles us, and let us run with endurance the race that is set before us" (Hebrews 12:1). The author of Hebrews portrays a distance race set by God which we are to run with endurance, remembering the faithful who ran before, and repenting of encumbrances that hold you back.

Endurance is one of the "waiting" words we examined in Chapter 1. You cannot run a marathon the same way you run a 40-yard dash. God does not call us to an explosion of good intentions in the starting blocks, but a plodding, diligent faithfulness over the long haul. If you haven't learned how to rest your body and your mind in appropriate seasons, you're not going to be able to run with endurance. Some need to learn what Jesus means about finding "rest for your souls" in Him. There is a rest for mankind that God intends, and it is centered in the person and work of Jesus His Son.

Furious activity is not the same thing as diligence. In fact, it can be counterproductive. Sleeping is good—at the right time, and for the right reasons. Go to bed, get horizontal, put your head on the pillow, and say, "I'm going to sleep, and I'm going to sleep well and I'm going to sleep long; I will be as thorough and diligent in my sleeping as I am in everything else so that I can wake up in the morning and run for Jesus." Learn to rest to run long.

8. We Will Have Rest When We Die—For Now We Work for the Lord

In 2001, my wife and I spent a couple weeks with a friend in another country. At the time, English-speaking Americans were something of an attraction, and my friend used us (and our entourage of college students) as a draw for gospel conversations. We spent 12 to 14 hours a day, day after day, speaking the gospel to lines of people who were eager to converse with us. Evangelizing through translation to seemingly endless listeners was thrilling and exhausting. When the alarm sounded for our pre-sunrise wakening, every member of our team wondered how we would have strength to get through this new day. My friend repeated to our team (until we were really as tired of hearing him say it as we were tired of waking up tired), "We will have rest when we die. For now, we work for the Lord."

This is a mantra that still echoes in my heart and reflects something Paul said to the Corinthian Christians: "Therefore, my beloved brethren, be steadfast, immovable, always abounding in the work of the Lord, knowing that your toil is not in vain in the Lord" (1 Corinthians 15:58). Toil for Jesus is not in vain. At the risk of appearing to contradict what was just said about a marathon, some of us need to be reminded that next to eternity, life is short (James 4:14), and you only get one shot (Hebrews 9:27). What are you doing with this evaporating moment known as your earthly existence? Paul tells us to be immovable rocks of conviction, tireless in our labor, and mindful of our reward. Work hard for Him; it will not be in vain.

9. Work at Faith

Faith is no idle task. Peter did not believe that faith was just a matter of sitting around believing stuff.

Now for this very reason also, applying all diligence, in your faith supply moral excellence, and in your moral excellence, knowledge, and in your knowledge, self-control, and in your self-control, perseverance, and in your perseverance, godliness, and in your godliness, brotherly kindness, and in your brotherly kindness, love. For if these qualities are yours and are increasing, they render you neither useless nor unfruitful in the true knowledge of our Lord Jesus Christ. For he who lacks these qualities is blind or short-sighted, having forgotten his purification from his former sins. Therefore, brethren, be all the more diligent to make certain about His calling and choosing you; for as long as you practice these things, you will never stumble; for in this way the entrance into the eternal kingdom of our Lord and Savior Jesus Christ will be abundantly supplied to you (2 Peter 1:5-11).

This is the work-ethic of Proverbs applied to faith in Jesus. If you want to eat in the fall, plant in the spring. If you want to grow in your faith in and knowledge of Jesus Christ, apply diligence in the disciplines that produce growth. Charles Bridges wrote, "Faith without diligence is slumbering delusion."[14] Waiting on God is a disposition of faith that produces obedience. Laziness is not to be credited as biblical waiting. Rather, waiting on God means doing what God says to do when we should do it and trusting Him with the results.

---

14 Charles Bridges, *A Commentary on Proverbs* (Edinburgh: The Banner of Truth Trust, 1981), 62.

WAITING
FOR JESUS

Waiting for Jesus is the heart of biblical waiting. Old Testament history was a four-thousand-year wait for Jesus. Two more millennia have elapsed since He first appeared, and once again, God's people wait. We wait for the return of Jesus.

Imagine, for a moment, an ordinary day. You wake up, start the coffee, and pour your Cheerios into a bowl. You tie your shoes, get into your car, and head to work. You greet your coworkers, inhabit your cubicle, and start accomplishing things. A message arrives at your desk. A nondescript envelope contains a simple message: you have been declared a citizen of a country you've never heard of.

As you scour Wikipedia, you discover a land that somehow evaded your notice in seventh grade geography class. Remote, with a bustling economy and no crime, this previously unnoticed country is at peace within and without. An idyllic climate and natural beauty make this land the envy of every vacation brochure ever printed. As you read on, you discover that this country has a very strict immigration policy: no immigration. The only entrance into this country is by birth, and you are not qualified. You take another look at the announcement you received; you have been declared a citizen.

As your research continues, you discover that the greatest asset of this far-off land is its king. An absolute monarch with no rival, his word goes, and nobody argues. But his word is good. His governance produces maximum benefit for every citizen at the expense of none. Every one of his subjects prospers under his good and kind reign.

Imagine the thoughts that would flood your mind as you looked up from your research to survey your surroundings: the desk, the cubicle, your coworkers. Your life has immediately and fundamentally been altered. This little announcement would, from then on, change the way you would eat your cereal, tie your shoes, go to work, and spend time with your friends. This would change the manner in which you make money, go to school, select a career, choose a spouse, and raise your kids. A note like that at your desk would be life-transforming.

Christian, you need not imagine. This is your narrative, your story. This is precisely what has happened to you already. Paul delivered just such a note to the believers in the church at Philippi: "For our citizenship is in heaven, from which also we eagerly wait for a Savior, the Lord Jesus Christ; who will transform the body of our humble state into conformity with the body of His glory, by the exertion of the power that He has even to subject all things to Himself" (Philippians 3:20–21). This announcement in Philippians 3 provides several reminders that ought to affect the way we live every moment of our earthly existence: we belong to heaven, we wait for Jesus, and we will be changed.

Before we can investigate this remarkable declaration, we need to observe its context. The Apostle Paul introduces this life-altering announcement in Philippians 3:20 with the simple conjunction "for," indicating a connection to verses 17 to 19. He traces a contrast between the eternal perspective of verses 20 and 21 and the temporal-mindedness of so-called Christians in the preceding verses.

> Brethren, join in following my example, and observe those who walk according to the pattern you have in us. For many walk, of whom I often told you, and now tell you even weeping, that they are enemies of the cross of Christ, whose end is destruction, whose god is their appetite, and whose glory is in their shame, who set their minds on earthly things (Philippians 3:17–19).

Paul encourages the Philippians to follow his example and the example of others who have followed Jesus well. What had they seen in Paul's life? Joy while suffering for Christ. The Christian's joy does not originate in this life; rather, his joy is found in Christ, because the Christian's life is in Him. Paul walked in stark contrast to the professing Christians described in verse 18. "For many walk, of whom I often told you, and now tell you even weeping, that they are enemies of the cross of Christ." Overrun by temporal thinking, these so-called Christians are said to "walk," yet they are "enemies of the cross of Christ," whose "god is their appetite." Believers could be tempted to imitate people who say they love Jesus with their lips but love the world with their hearts. James tells us that "friendship with the world is hostility toward God" (James 4:4). The possibility that genuine Christians at Philippi might imbibe this temporal-mindedness grieved Paul. He pleaded with the Philippians through tears not to follow their example.

These worldly insiders are particularly dangerous because they profess affiliation to Jesus. By contrast, professed unbelievers, having no interest in Christ or the church, do not pose the same insidious threat to Christians. But Paul warns the Philippians of these Christians-in-name-only. Their worldview and theology are entirely temporal. Notice the remarkable way Paul describes them, "Their end is destruction." The trajectory of their kind of living terminates in the lake of fire. They are "enemies of the cross of Christ." He doesn't just say that they are enemies of the gospel; they are enemies of the cross of Christ, a reference to the very suffering that purchased believers' redemption. What cross-less message do false teachers peddle? A "gospel" without suffering, a Christianity without the cross, without the death of Christ and the hardships of being His followers. Such a message is not true Christianity. False teachers can sell moralism, prosperity, or a better life now, but this is not the message that Paul preached. This is not the message of Jesus. Genuine Christianity offers a gospel of deferred gratification. The Christian's earthly pilgrimage is a walk of waiting. The false professors at Philippi promoted a "gospel" of immediate gratification.

There is more to the agenda of these false teachers, and it is found in what they worship. Their god is their appetite—what they want, when they want it. Paul strips the thin veneer of their Christian lingo to reveal a secret idolatry that drives all of life. Tragically, their glory is in their shame. These so-called Christians have exchanged the glory of the immortal God for temporal enjoyments. They found an ability to reprogram their consciences and actually live in the things that ought to bring shame. Instead of boasting they knew God (Jeremiah 9:24), they seem to have boasted in their sin. They "set their minds on earthly things." They have an under-the-sun perspective; for them the carpe diem refrain compels them: eat, drink and be merry, for tomorrow we'll die. They have been deceived into thinking they can put most of their eggs in the basket of this world and still have an interest in Jesus. Paul tells the Philippians, "don't follow them."

There is a warning here against following the current Christian infatuation with so-called "freedoms." Large segments of professing Christians today seem to want to be known for the edgy behaviors in which they feel free to participate. Unfettered in their minds by the deception that God's grace provides license, and seeking to prove their deep understanding of "grace," they become enslaved to the very appetites that will destroy them. They act as though the grace of God in the gospel of Jesus is a license to indulge temporal appetites. Rather, the grace of God teaches us to deny ungodliness (Titus 2:12), because the grace which invades our lives by the gospel is not merely the disposition of God to be kind to undeserving sinners; it is also the power of God to transform them. God is doubly kind to us through gospel-grace: He forgives our sinning, and He provides power for righteousness. Far from being merely a feeling in God toward sinners, grace is the power of God to dominate the Christian's earthly existence for the promotion of lived-out righteousness. "Grace… [reigns] through righteousness to eternal life through Jesus Christ our Lord" (Romans 5:21). Are you known more for your temporal appetites or for a grace-driven longing for eternal realities? Would Paul commend your life as an example to be followed, or as a life to be grieved over and avoided?

The Apostle Paul encouraged the Philippian believers to follow his own example, living as belonging to another realm. Philippians 3:20-21 unfolds the reason for this instruction, three realities which radically alter our earthly pilgrimage, beginning with this statement of the Christian's identity: "our citizenship is in heaven."

We Belong to Heaven

The first reality that ought to radically change our earthly existence is that heaven is our home. You are a registered citizen of a place you've never been. The only place you've ever known is a land in which you do not belong.

In 49 BC, all Italians were Roman citizens. By 47 AD, just under a century later, only nine percent of all the people living in the Roman Empire were actual Roman citizens. Citizenship in the Roman Empire was a prized commodity. Some were born into citizenship, and some purchased it at a high price. Roman citizenship came with privileges, esteem, recognition, rights and protections.

In the vast empire, the city of Philippi was a privileged city. Originally colonized by war veterans who were honored Roman citizens, Philippi was constituted by Octavius as a "Little Rome," a copy of the great city, patterned after home. So in a seaside outpost in Greece nearly 600 miles away from Rome, a settlement of Roman citizens established a way of life that reflected the values, governance, and beauty of the city to which they belonged. By the time Paul wrote this letter to the church at Philippi, many of the city's citizens had never even been to Rome. Yet their citizenship and their livelihood belonged to that city they had never seen.

What we Christians have in our citizenship in heaven is better than what citizens of Philippi had in relationship to Rome. We are not just a provincial outpost that resembles our home. God has "seated us with Him in the heavenly places in Christ Jesus" (Ephesians 2:6) and has "rescued us from the domain of darkness, and transferred us to the kingdom of His beloved Son" (Colossians 1:13). Our citizenship, governance, identity, passions, and priorities are those of heaven. Notice that Paul does not say, "your citizenship will be in heaven." Our citizenship *is* in heaven. This is a present reality, causing us to feel homesick for our permanent residence. We therefore ought to long to be governed by the priorities and directives of the home to which we belong.

How does one become a citizen of heaven? Only by birth and

blood. Jesus told Nicodemus, "you must be born again" (John 3:3-5), and He spilled His own blood to purchase our citizenship. Christianity is not just a different way to live. You cannot get in by cleaning up your life and dragging around a new bag of self-made morality. God despises man-made forgeries of the righteousness required to be in His presence. He will only accept the righteousness that He Himself provides through the blood spilt by His own Son. Only blood-bought, born-again followers of Jesus belong to heaven.

Are you homesick for your permanent residence? Are you now being governed by the priorities and the passions of Heaven? Did you receive that little announcement that declared you a citizen of another land? Do you read and reread that declaration every day? Does that declaration change the flavor of your breakfast and dictate the way you make your friends and raise your kids and go to work and make plans? Heaven is home. That is a present reality for the follower of Jesus Christ. Our citizenship is a reality that must flavor every moment of our earthly existence.

We Wait for Jesus

There is a second reality in Philippians 3:20 that gives us cause to live for eternity rather than for the fulfillment of temporal appetites: we wait for Jesus. "For our citizenship is in heaven, from which also we eagerly wait for a Savior, the Lord Jesus Christ." The word translated "we eagerly wait" appears eight times in the New Testament, and it is eschatological in every context. It refers to the end of time when Jesus sets everything right. To wait for Jesus is to live in eager anticipation, longing for the end when Jesus wins, when Jesus is vindicated, and when His people shine. Paul says that the Christian's citizenship is in heaven, "from which we eagerly wait for a Savior, the Lord Jesus

Christ." Our home is in heaven, and our Savior will come from heaven. Heaven is home because Jesus is there. We long for heaven because we love our King, and we wait in eager expectation until everything that is home for us is realized in its fullness.

Notice the designation that is given to Jesus: "Savior, the Lord Jesus Christ." He is Savior. The Bible describes our salvation in numerous ways, with a past component, a present reality, and a future consummation. We have been saved, we are being saved, and we will be saved. This verse is a reference to that future reality. We will have been saved from God's punishment, by God's power, unto God's presence. We await a Savior who comes to fulfill and finalize our salvation, ushering us into the glorious reality of the unmediated presence of God. Jesus also is called the Lord. He is the sovereign master of the universe, and He is in charge of every Christian's life personally. This savior and lord is called Jesus. He became a baby at Bethlehem to die at Calvary to bring us to God. He is Savior, the Lord Jesus, the Christ. "Christ," of course, is not Jesus' last name; it is His title, the Greek word for Messiah. This Jesus is the one for whom humanity waited 4,000 years. He is the anointed One, the expected One, the God-Man. Only a man could die, but only God could satisfy the infinite wrath of God to pay for sin. Our Savior, the Lord Jesus Christ, came to earth, died on a cross, rose from the dead, ascended to the right hand of the Father, intercedes on our behalf, and will return to make all things right. This is the One for whom we eagerly wait.

We Will Be Changed

Paul presents in verse 21 a third life-altering reality: Jesus will change us. The Lord Jesus Christ "will transform the body of our humble state into conformity with the body of His glory, by the exertion of the power that He has even to subject all things to Himself."

You are not now what you will be, and you cannot go home in your present condition. The realm for which you been secured by new birth and Jesus' blood is perfect. And you, in your current state, are not. If you went to heaven unchanged, heaven would cease to be what it is. You and I must be transformed. Believers look forward to this promised change, because it will make us fit to enjoy the full benefits of our citizenship. Jesus Himself will finish what He has begun in us, transforming the body of our humiliation into conformity with His glorious resurrection body.

Listen to the way Paul describes this transformation in 1 Corinthians 15:

> So also is the resurrection of the dead. It is sown a perishable body, it is raised an imperishable body; it is sown in dishonor, it is raised in glory; it is sown in weakness, it is raised in power; it is sown a natural body, it is raised a spiritual body.... However, the spiritual is not first, but the natural; then the spiritual. The first man is from the earth, earthy; the second man is from heaven. As is the earthy, so also are those who are earthy; and as is the heavenly, so also are those who are heavenly. Just as we have borne the image of the earthy, we will also bear the image of the heavenly. Now I say this, brethren, that flesh and blood cannot inherit the kingdom of God; nor does the perishable inherit the imperishable. Behold, I tell you a mystery; we will not all sleep, but we will all be changed, in a moment, in the twinkling of an eye, at the last trumpet; for the trumpet will sound, and the dead will be raised imperishable, and we will be changed. For this perishable must put on the imperish-

able, and this mortal must put on immortality (1 Corinthians 15:42-53).

You and I cannot be the heirs of the realm for which we are destined, if we remain as we are. Things must change drastically. Mortality must be replaced by immortality; weakness and decay must give way to power and invincibility. The natural and earthy must step aside for the supernatural and heavenly. We are not physically fit yet for our homeland. We must wait for transformation.

Beside our physical frailty, we are currently plagued by spiritual weakness that makes us unfit for heaven. While believers in Jesus Christ are not what they once were, they are also not what they will be. We live in a mixed condition, with two natures. Before you were born again, you possessed one nature, living in unmixed spiritual deadness. When you were made alive by the Spirit of God at regeneration, that old unmixed condition passed away, and a new condition emerged: a mixed condition. You now possess spiritual life to go along with your residual sinfulness. The Christian on earth has the capacity to sin and the capacity to please God. This mixed condition with two natures, even with all of the internal conflict it affords, is far better than the unmixed condition you lived in before you knew Jesus. Yet there is another condition to which we look forward: the unmixed condition of untainted conformity to Jesus! Until the Christian reflects Jesus without the stain of residual sin, he cannot dwell in his eternal home. The Christian must wait for the coming transformation.

Jesus Himself will accomplish the required transformation. How will He do this? Jesus "will transform the body of our humble state into conformity with the body of His glory, by the exertion of the power that He has even to subject all things to Himself" (Philippians

3:21). The "all things" here includes all the natural and supernatural enemies of God, which Jesus possesses the power to vanquish.

Consider the number and strength of Jesus' enemies. Like bad clay in the hands of a potter, rebellious humans fight against the good designs of their Creator. Rebels use God's air to utter blasphemies, rail complaints while standing on His earth, and build idols with His materials. The pinnacle of His creation, made in His image in order to reflect His glory and display His goodness, have squandered their many gifts and failed at their most basic reason for existing.

Aside from rebellious humans, a world of spiritual enemies also opposes its Maker. Satan and his hordes have spent six millennia making war against God. That fallen angel, chief of God's enemies, is the prince of the power of the air, and he is at work in the sons of disobedience. He has at every turn attempted to thwart God's plan and frustrate His purposes. He has lied, blasphemed, and murdered. He is powerful, and he has set his sights particularly on the destruction of mankind. Even my own residual sinfulness lends its help to the powerful alliance of the world and the devil.

What kind of power will it take to subjugate the enemies of God? What will it take to silence every rebellious tongue? More than that, what kind of power is required to make every rebellious tongue actually confess that Jesus is Lord? What would it take to make every enemy knee bow to the one true God? What will it take to tame my tongue and tether my affections? Jesus will do it! The same One who will level all mountains, burn up the universe, and create a new heaven and a new earth, is the same one who will subjugate everything to His glory and His honor. He will vindicate His name. Every knee will bow and every tongue will confess that He is Lord to the glory of the Father. He alone is able to subjugate everything under His rulership.

And He, with that same power, will transform our body of humiliation into conformity with His glorious body.

Jesus possesses the unparalleled power of making His detractors comply. The fact that He does not do it yet causes some to doubt whether He possesses such power. (And whether they realize it or not, Jesus' enemies even now are stooges on short leashes, only able to accomplish His plan!) Make no mistake, Jesus can and Jesus will make every one of them confess and bow. And the power Jesus owns to subject everything to Himself is the power He will use to transform the body of our humble state into conformity with the body of His glory.

Christians anticipate an exciting future: heaven is home, and we're waiting for Jesus, the glorious king, to make us fit for entrance into our permanent residence. These are realities that ought to change the way we eat our cereal, tie our shoes, go to work, and raise our kids. Nothing is more clarifying than the contemplation of eternal realities.

What will heaven be like? For the full answer to that question, the Christian must wait. But Scripture provides some teasers, enough to cement in our minds the conviction that heaven will not be boring! Rather, the essence of heaven will be the infinitely increasing delight of discovering the radiating glories of the infinite Fountain of treasure—God Himself!

For one glimpse of the incredible future awaiting the believer, it will be helpful to revisit a passage we looked at in Chapter 4. In Luke 12, Jesus instructed His followers to wait for His return like slaves awaiting their master's return at night.

> Be dressed in readiness, and keep your lamps lit. Be like men who are waiting for their master when he returns from the wedding feast, so that they may immediately open the door to him when he comes and knocks. Blessed are those slaves whom the master

will find on the alert when he comes; truly I say to you, that he will gird himself to serve, and have them recline at the table, and will come up and wait on them. Whether he comes in the second watch, or even in the third, and finds them so, blessed are those slaves (Luke 12:35–38).

In chapter 4, we skipped over verse 37, but we need to revisit this verse in order to get a flavor of what is in store for those who are waiting for Jesus. Jesus tells a story in Luke 12:35-38 about how to wait for His return, illustrated by slaves waiting for their master to return from a wedding feast at night. They were to be belted in readiness, lamps lit, obedient, eager to open the door when he comes, ready to serve their master.

Jesus' story takes a surprising turn in verse 37: "Blessed are those slaves whom the master will find on the alert when he comes; truly I say to you, that he will gird himself to serve, and have them recline at the table, and will come up and wait on them." Who is the master in this story? Jesus. Who in this story will recline at the table and be served? The slaves. Who in this story is dressed and ready to serve? Jesus! This is shocking! We should not believe the message of this parable if it were not spoken by God Himself. No master leaves his slaves in charge to keep the house ready so that when he returns he can come through the door, put on his slave clothes, and serve them. And that is exactly what Jesus says the master will do when he returns to the house.

If we knew our God well, this remarkable reversal might not be so surprising. The owner of the universe, when He walked on His own green earth, said, "The Son of Man did not come to be served but to serve and to give His life as a ransom for many" (Matthew 20:28). He created, sustained, and tolerated earth-dwelling rebels so that He might rescue, transform, and bring some of them home to His heavenly kingdom. He will make them inheritors of His kingdom, and He will wait on them.

God has always been the servant of His creatures in order to put His own attributes on display. The essence of heaven will be the creature's experience of the excellencies of God. We will revel in who He is. God's attributes do not change from time to eternity. He doesn't stop being gracious, giving, selfless, kind, or overflowing in love when eternity starts. He doesn't stop being an endless fountain that pours out goodness upon goodness upon goodness to people who don't deserve to have any taste of it. And the self-giving nature of God will overflow into countless eons multiplied by infinite ages. This is who our God is. He is good, abounding in lovingkindness for those who love Him. This is precisely the reality for which He has constructed time and space and eternity. Taste and see that the Lord is good!

Heaven is too good to be true! And yet it is true. God will give and give and give of Himself to miserable wretches who surrendered their earthly lives to Him. It is true for all who wait on Him, who have found joy in suffering for Him. This is the reward for those who have preferred the deferred gratification of waiting on Jesus to the empty vanities of temporal treasure. If you have Jesus, you have everything. Wait on the Lord, and He will wait on you.

God loves our family
and wants us to
love each other.